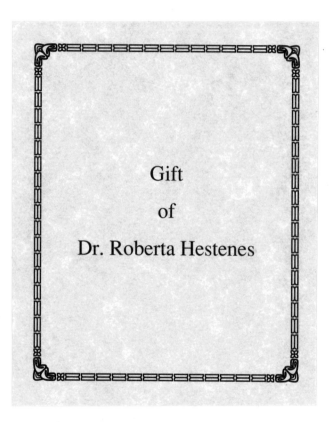

THE
DILEMMA
OF
DEVELOPMENT

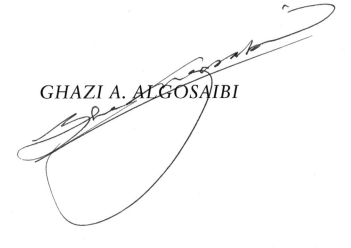

GHAZI A. ALGOSAIBI

THE
DILEMMA
OF
DEVELOPMENT

Translated from the Arabic
by Leslie McLoughlin

First English Edition

ISBN: 0 86372 188 5

British Library Cataloguing-in-Publication Data
A catalogue record for this book is available from the British Library

Jacket design by David Rose and Mark Slader
Jacket photograph courtesy of Jean-Pierre Ribière, *Sudan, The Passing of
Time*, Garnet Publishing, 1994
Typeset by Sarah Golden
Printed in Lebanon

Typeset in 11/14 Sabon

Ithaca Press is an imprint of Garnet Publishing

Published by Garnet Publishing Ltd,
8 Southern Court, South Street,
Reading, RG1 4QS, UK

CONTENTS

PREFACE

Whenever a new regime comes to power in the Third World, 'Communiqué No. 1' generously promises the masses a better life, i.e. development. Whenever a Third World government boasts of the stability which it has achieved, it means that it has achieved prosperity through stability, i.e. development. When the communist regimes of Eastern Europe fell after monopolizing power for forty years, their downfall was due to the economic straitjacket they had imposed on their citizens. Here too, the cause was linked to the lack of development. When the leader of the Soviet Union proclaimed the policies of 'glasnost' and 'perestroika', he did so because the shelves of Moscow's shops were empty even of meat and soap.

Without oversimplifying and ignoring the host of interrelated, and sometimes contradictory, factors which underlie every policy decision and every political stance, we can say that the issue of development has been at the root of every revolution which has taken place over the past hundred years. And every counter-revolution too. The leaders of the abortive coup against Gorbachev in August 1991 sought to justify their actions by saying that their aim was to correct the policies which had brought the Soviet people to the point of starvation. In other words, development has been and remains the key issue of the twentieth century.

Over the past half century, an enormous body of literature has emerged, to constitute what we might call 'development sciences'. Thus, development has become a discipline in its own right, taught at universities, studied at specialist research centres, discussed at seminars and conferences and expressed in its own metalanguage. There are those – a majority – who study development from a purely economic point of view; others consider the political aspects; others focus on the psychological factors; still others analyse the sociological elements.

Is it possible that this little book can add anything to the wealth of information on development produced by researchers in the West and in the East? I doubt it very much. So, why write it? Well, I studied some aspects of development at university, then went on to lecture on the subject and eventually found myself responsible for certain development issues, first as Minister of Industry and Electricity and later as Minister of Health, in my own society. Throughout these years, I found the prospect of reading any book on development almost as painful as a visit to the dentist. The reason is simple: almost all such books are written by specialists for specialists. Confronted with a variety of mathematical symbols, formulae, tables and statistics, the general reader is hard put to find anything that he can understand or recognize in the real world. Hence, the inspiration for this book: a discussion of development in terms which can be understood by the non-specialist and to bring the study of development back to its roots in humanity.

The first test for independent development is to find answers to the following four questions:

1. Why do we strive to develop?
2. For whom do we strive to develop?
3. What do we develop?
4. How do we develop?[1]

I shall attempt to answer these questions in the following pages.

NOTE

1   Yusuf Sa'igh, 'Towards Independent Development in the Arab World' in *Independent Development in the Arab World*, Beirut, Centre for Arab Unity Studies, 1987, p. 992.

CHAPTER 1

WHY DO WE
STRIVE TO DEVELOP?

We have honoured the sons
Of Adam; provided them
With transport on land and sea;
Given them for sustenance things
Good and pure; and conferred
On them special favours,
Above a great part
Of Our Creation.

The Qur'an

WHY DO WE
STRIVE TO DEVELOP?

Development terminology poses a difficult problem. At first, the term 'backward' was used to describe countries which still lacked the bases for development. With the advent of independence and national pride, however, the old term was swept aside and replaced by a new word, 'underdeveloped'. When it then became apparent that this adjective took no account of the real and serious efforts being made for development in these countries, they came to be described as 'developing'. 'Countries of the Third World', is a term now gaining currency in the literature, and I have opted for it in this study as it covers countries at different levels of development. By 'First World', I mean countries which have achieved development through capitalism; by 'Second World' or the Eastern bloc (now about to fade into history), I mean countries which have developed through socialism ; by 'Third World', I mean the countries of Asia, Africa and Latin America which are still struggling against the wretched conditions of backwardness.

In this book, development does not refer to some utopia which has never existed and never will. What we mean by development is a level of economic, social and political development which some countries have managed to achieve but not others.

The concept may be illustrated by comparing someone in an industrialized country with someone in a Third World country. Compare, say, an American from Georgia, a state famous for growing peanuts, with a citizen of Senegal, a country equally famous for this crop (the USA and Senegal are among the largest exporters of peanuts in the world). Let us see first how our American friend lives and then how his counterpart lives in Senegal.

John Johnston is 43 and farms 54 acres of peanuts. To prepare the soil, he uses sophisticated modern machinery. He benefits from scientific research funded by the government to select the best seeds and fertilizers. He also benefits from a programme of services for farmers, provided by the government, explaining the results of research in agronomy and the ways to make use of them. Johnston protects his crops by spraying them with pesticides from the air. At harvest time, he uses a combine which simultaneously gathers and shells the ripe peanuts.

Johnston sells his crop to a wholesaler in a neighbouring town, where the peanuts are stored under ultra-modern conditions. The crop is then sold on through other dealers in the state capital, Atlanta, and in New York and Chicago to companies which process and export the product. He gets paid more than the world market price for peanuts because the government intervenes to keep imports down, to limit the annual acreage cultivated and to protect farmers against fluctuations in the international markets.[1] Thus, the fact that Johnston achieves a yearly income of US$100,000 from his crop is due to a combination of factors: scientific research, modern machinery, effective marketing, government support and hard work. Out of this income, Johnston and his family can afford not only all the necessities of life but its luxuries as well.

What about our other friend, the Senegalese farmer? Shirno Sar grows peanuts on a small farm in the village of Jilab, which, like Johnston, he inherited from his father. The soil on Sar's farm is perfect for growing peanuts. He has just begun to introduce mechanical aids for ploughing and harvesting, processes which until recently were carried out manually. However, the equipment available to him is not of the same quality as that of his American counterpart. Our Senegalese friend cannot use fertilizers and pesticides, either because they are not available at all or because they cost too much. The result is that Sar harvests less than one-fifth of Johnston's crop.

When the harvest is in, Sar has no choice but to sell his crop to the State monopoly, which buys it for well under the international market price, thus ensuring that the government gets its share of the profit. The State monopoly then stores the crop under primitive conditions, with the result that a good percentage is lost due to vermin and exposure to the elements. Again, there is a combination of circumstances but, in this case, the situation is one of a small crop, low prices and losses in storage. Thus, Sar and his family of eight remain caught in the poverty trap and live on an income of US$400 per annum. Although they grow enough to feed themselves, the nutritional value of their food is below the minimum daily requirement. In Sar's village, there is no electricity, no school, no health centres and no shops. Sar's wife has to walk a long way from the family hut to fetch water. Out of every hundred children born in the village, only twenty are expected to live beyond their first year.

However, no one should delude himself for one moment that everyone in Senegal is as poor as Sar. In Dakar, the modern capital, the civil servants of the State monopoly responsible for the purchase and sale of peanuts work in air-conditioned offices, drive their own cars, live in comfortable houses and enjoy many of the same luxuries as the Johnstons in Georgia. Their children go to the best schools and are treated in modern hospitals. Still, the civil servants represent only a small minority of the population, a minority blessed by circumstances of birth, education and income at the expense of the overwhelming majority of small farmers. The peanuts grown in the village of Jilab are sold in the international market and the income they produce is used to pay these same civil servants salaries which far exceed the income of Sar and the other farmers of Jilab. It is also the income from the peanuts which serves to finance public services in the large towns far from Jilab and its poor farmers.

Now, what about the political environment surrounding our two friends in America and in Senegal? The congressman who represents Johnston in Washington is attentive to his needs and interests. The agricultural lobby carries a lot of clout on Capitol Hill, ensuring that the government maintains support for farm products, scientific research in agriculture and practical services to farmers. (All of this despite the fact that people working in agriculture represent only a small segment of America's industrial society.)

Sar, on the other hand, possesses no political influence whatever. There is no one to fight for his interests in the capital, despite the fact that the majority of the population consists of small farmers just like him. The urban minority alone has the ear of the government and enjoys its resources. Sar has no way of obtaining a better price for his crop or of putting pressure on the government to improve services to himself and his family.[2]

Needless to say, what has been said about Johnston goes for most citizens of every developed industrial country and, conversely, what has been said about Sar applies to most citizens of every country of the Third World.[3]

Perhaps we can now address the question of why we seek development. The answer is that we want a person like Sar to enjoy the same level of income and services as those enjoyed by his fellow human being, Johnston. It is not and must not be the aim of development to change Sar's name to Johnston, to make him speak in the same way, wear the same clothes, hold the same values and observe the same customs. It is not and must not be the aim of development to make Senegal part of the United States or to transplant American traditions to Senegal.

A supplementary question is: 'Why should we wish to make the social, economic and political environment of a citizen of the Third World comparable to that of a citizen of the First World?' The answer is simple. It would be morally reprehensible if development was not pursued to counter the evils of backwardness and poverty.[4] If development is not initiated, shocking differences will remain between peoples: 75 per cent of the world's wealth is presently concentrated in the hands of only 20 per cent of the total world population. If there is no development, the gap between rich and poor will continue to widen: since the Second World War, for every US$ that average per capita income has risen in the Third World, there has been a rise of US$286 in the First World. If no development takes place, famine will continue to claim its victims: every minute, throughout the world, abject poverty claims the lives of approximately twenty-five people.[5]

It would not be an exaggeration to say that, without successful and effective development, the Third World would suffer from devastating famines. The words may sound melodramatic but the figures speak for themselves and the story they have to tell is a horrifying one.

During the 1970s, the Third World received US$30 billion for exports of 12 basic commodities (excluding oil). These commodities were then processed in the First World and resold for a sum of US$200 billion. (For example, Third World cocoa farmers receive only about 10 per cent of the price of the chocolate it is made into in the First World.)

During the 1930s, the countries of the Third World exported about 10 million tonnes of cereals; during the 1950s, they were still self-sufficient; but by the end of the 1970s, they were importing around 70 million tonnes; by the end of the century, it is estimated that Third World imports of cereals will exceed 140 million tonnes.[6]

In 1988, Third World debt amounted to US$1,450 billion, while, in 1986, accrued interest and annual payments due on the debt came to approximately US$96 billion.[7]

In the final analysis, development is not an end in itself but a means to raise man's economic, social, political and cultural standards. Given this aim, anything which results in harm to man, in whatever way – physical or spiritual – can only impede development. Any change which does not serve man economically, socially, politically or culturally is one which has nothing to do with development. Thus, it is clear that the attempts which have been and are still being made in many countries of the Third World to obliterate their identity, to distort their individuality and to import beliefs and ideas from outside are destructive and divorced from the aims of true development.

With no clear vision and no well-defined priorities, development has been reduced to little more than a desperate attempt to provide a veneer for the Third World.

> With no sense of responsibility, the Third World seems intent on selling its cultural identity along with the greater part of its material wealth in exchange for a few skyscrapers and modern hospitals to cater for the needs of a small urban élite and for technology purchased with enormous loans to give a mirror image of the alien cultures which have produced them. For the unfortunate masses who live far from these modern facilities, economic development means nothing more than plastic containers, cheap and shoddy textiles, flimsy and temporary housing, mounting external debt and, from time to time, handouts from central government in the form of food subsidies.[8]

The downward spiral started when political leaders imagined that change for its own sake meant development. The first political leader to champion this line of thought was Mustafa Kemal Atatürk. He believed that development meant changing the identity of Turkey from an oriental Islamic State to a secular European one and he waged all-out war on anything connected with the heritage, customs and traditions of his country. Atatürk prohibited Turkish men from wearing the fez and used military force to stop women from wearing the veil. He suppressed the use of Arabic script to write Turkish and replaced it with the Roman alphabet. Not even in the West, which Atatürk so idolized, was Islam persecuted with the same ferocity as in Turkey, which had for so many centuries been its foremost bastion.

Under Shah Reza Khan, the father of Muhammad Reza Pahlevi, Iran went the same way as Turkey under Atatürk. The Shah banned the wearing of traditional Iranian clothes and commanded that everyone should wear a hat. Women were forbidden to wear the *shadur* and the police were instructed to rip it off the back of any woman found wearing one in public. When people gathered in their mosques to protest, artillery was brought in. The Shah ordered the nomadic tribes to be settled against their wishes and, when they resisted, he sent in the army to subdue them and ordered their wells to be poisoned. He banned pictures of camels, which were seen as beasts serving a primitive economy and symbolizing backwardness![9]

An objective observer might legitimately ask what forcing men to wear hats, forcing women to discard the *shadur*, poisoning wells and banning pictures of camels had to do with development? Did these bizarre measures lead to any development worth mentioning? The result was the emergence of a class bitterly satirized by Ali Shariati, one of Iran's intellectuals, in the following parody of one of its members:

> He tried desperately to get his grandmother, Hajja Bibi Kalban Agha, to wear a miniskirt to go out or to tie her hair in a pony-tail. He tried to persuade his aunt, Hajja Ruqaya,

to wear Audrey Hepburn glasses. He cleared the house of the rugs, mats and cushions which had been in the family for sixty years so that he could refurnish it in the modern American style he had seen in 'Burda'. A poster of Jayne Mansfield, intended for the bedroom, was put up in his parents' house on the wall his pious father used to face when praying![10]

True leaders who are close to the hearts and minds of their people instinctively realize that development cannot be imposed on the masses by *diktat* from above and that their needs, customs and traditions cannot be ignored. On this subject, I recall the late Indira Gandhi telling me:

It is the people themselves who must decide the pace of change they want. The pace can't be dictated by government. Even when the level of public awareness is low, we have to rely on patience and persuasion. In India, for example, when the government built a dam to control flooding and generate electricity, members of the opposition went about telling people from the neighbouring villages that the dam had robbed the water of its spirit. They convinced the villagers that the water was no longer blessed and so was unsuitable for irrigation. I didn't think that anyone could fall for such a tale. Yet, unbelievable as it may seem, during my visits to the area, several people came up to me and asked: 'Why have you robbed the water of its spirit?' or 'Why have you left the water without any blessing?' Faced with questions like that, what is there that one can do? The only solution is to be patient and to persuade.[11]

One cannot forget the enormous price Indira Gandhi had to pay when, for a time, she ignored her own maxim and tried to 'encourage' men to accept the sterilization programme which formed part of her family planning campaign. That initiative was one of the main reasons she was voted out of power in 1977.

Why do we strive to develop? Because underdevelopment – and the poverty that goes with it – is not the preordained lot of man. Whatever the causes may be, there is nothing that an enlightened approach and determination cannot solve. Though scholars have tried to explain the phenomenon of underdevelopment in various ways, they are all agreed that it is not an incurable disease. Some experts take the view that geographical factors are to blame. Others hold that it is a scourge for which political systems are mainly responsible. A third group believes that the problem lies in the type of economic system adopted. There are also those who have tried to distinguish between various kinds of backwardness. One of the best known of these taxonomies was drawn up by the famous American economist, J. K. Galbraith, who discerned three categories. According to him, underdevelopment in Asia was due to a lack of natural resources, i.e. too many people chasing too few natural resources. For Africa, he put underdevelopment down to a lack of human resources, i.e. the Africans were not educated or trained in a way which would enable them to exploit the natural resources available to them. As for Latin America, Galbraith took the view that underdevelopment there derived not from any lack of natural or human resources but, rather, from the shortcomings of social, economic and political institutions.[12]

The scholars and writers who have addressed the issue of backwardness and development did not start out on their research from nowhere, nor did they have no destination in mind. They have all approached the issue on the basis of postulates which they themselves have formulated and they have all arrived at the conclusions they had hoped to reach. This rule applies equally to those who approached the issue from a particular religious standpoint which coloured their view and analysis of the subject, to those whose starting-point was a political system which they sought to apply, and to those who adopted a scientific approach, with no prejudice in favour of a particular doctrine or political credo.[13] They have all written about development out of the firm belief that it is a goal which can be achieved. Gone too are the racist theories which singled out one people as having the genius, intelligence and ability to break free of the yoke of poverty but excluded others. Even those who still whisper that the true cause of underdevelopment is laziness would do well to note the remark of the eminent Western scholar, A. G. Frank:

> It is clear that underdevelopment is not a question of a lazy disposition or the espousal of strange values. On the contrary, throughout the period of colonialism, black slaves carried out tasks which were a great deal harder than any work ever done by their masters . . . Even today, a great many people in the non-developed world, young and old, have to work a lot harder than people in the developed world, just to survive.[14]

A further answer to the question 'why do we seek to develop?' is that man's destiny should be to live in dignity.[15] Much has already been done in the Third World to enhance it. In the period between 1960 and 1987, life expectancy in the Third World climbed from 46 to 62. Adult literacy rose from 43 to 60 per cent. The death rate among children under five was reduced by half, while the provision of health care services was extended to about 61 per cent of the population.[16] So much for what has been achieved.

The picture is still very bleak in many respects: illiteracy remains widespread, with about a billion people unable to read or write; some 2 billion people are without potable water; another 100 million individuals live with no roof over their heads; 800 million people go to bed hungry every night; some

150 million children suffer from malnutrition and 14 million of them die before the age of five.[17]

The road which leads towards development and the dignity which man deserves remains a long and hard one.

Notes

1   It is naïvely believed by some in the Third World that the govern-ments of free market States never intervene in the economies of their countries. The truth of the matter, of course, is that they intervene in a thousand and one ways! There is, however, a big difference between intelligent intervention and the hit-and-miss control practised in most Third World countries.

2   For a comparison between the American and the Senegalese farmer, see Malcolm Gillis *et al.*, *Economics of Development*, New York, W. W. Norton & Co., 1983, pp. 3–5.

3   In 1987, per capita income in the Third World averaged only 6 per cent of per capita income in the First World. Whereas average per capita income in Germany was around US$18,000 p.a., the figure for Bangladesh was US$174.

4   'You shall not go hungry or naked. You shall not thirst or want for shade.' Thus was Adam first given God's assurance that he would not have to suffer poverty. He was clothed and fed and, when the time came to leave the Garden, these rights remained in the forefront of Adam's consciousness. See Khalid Muhammad Khalid, *Islaamiyaat*, Beirut, Dar al-Fikr, AH1398/AD1978, p. 12.

5   See Richard W. Lombardi, *Debt Trap: Rethinking the Logic of Development*, New York, Praeger, 1985, p. xviii.

6   Ibid., p. 34.

7   See Ramzi Zaki, 'Cancelling Third World Debt is a Necessity not an Option', *al-Arabi*, Nov. 1989, p. 26.

8   Lombardi, op. cit., p. 7

9   See Rysyard Karuscinski, *Shah of Shahs*, London, Quartet Books, 1985, p. 3.

10 Ali Shariati, *Return to Self*, trans. by Ibrahim al-Dasuqi Shatta, Cairo, al-Zahra li'l-I'lam al-Arabi, first edn., 1986, pp. 111–12.

11 From a discussion with the author during an official visit to Saudi Arabia in the spring of 1982.

12 André Gunder Frank, *Critique and Anti-Critique*, New York, Praeger, 1984, p. 90.

13 Nath Verma Baidya, *The Sociology and Politics of Development*, London, Routledge & Kegan Paul, 1980.

14 A. G. Frank, op. cit., p. 91.

15 Islam guarantees man 'the right to self-sufficiency, i.e. a decent living standard for every individual in terms of food, clothing, housing, education, medical care and leisure'. See Muhammad Shawqi al-Fanjari, 'Man's right under Islam to a decent standard of living', *Human Rights Journal*, 8/7 (1990), pp. 45–52.

16 See *Human Development Report 1990*, published for the UNDP by Oxford University Press, New York, p. 2.

17 Ibid., p. 2.

CHAPTER 2

FOR WHOM DO WE STRIVE TO DEVELOP?

What God has bestowed
On His Apostle (and taken
Away) from the people
Of the townships, belongs
To God, to His Apostle
And to kindred and orphans,
The needy and the wayfarer;
In order that it may not
(Merely) be a monopoly
of the wealthy among you.

The Qur'an

FOR WHOM DO
WE STRIVE TO DEVELOP?

The question itself would have seemed very strange indeed had it been asked a century or even half a century ago. At that time, the vogue word was 'growth' and no one ever spoke about 'development'. At the time, scholars had not yet realized that there was a big difference between spontaneous and unstructured 'growth' and deliberately planned 'development'. The philosophy of growth was crystal clear: it was growth and growth alone which served the interest of society as a whole and there was no reason to look any further. Should any further questions be asked, the answer would come back that, given time, the benefits of growth would 'trickle down' to all classes in society and that even the poorest of them would benefit. The rationale for growth followed classical economic theory which held that man had only to maximize profits and minimize losses and, provided everyone adopted this approach, everyone would benefit at the end of the day.

However, in practice, things did not move along in this comfortable manner. True, there was growth but development did not always follow. True, there was prosperity, but not everyone prospered. True, the rich became richer, but the poor also became poorer. The old answers are no longer convincing.

The Poverty Curtain, an excellent study by the well-known Pakistani economist, Mahboub Alhaq, describes the long and bitter transition from growth to development. He tells how he started out on his professional career as a believer in growth, which he planned on behalf of the government of Pakistan, and how he ended as a convert to development, proselytizing for it within the World Bank. He explains the enormous difference between growth, which benefits only the few, and development, which is carried out for the benefit of the broad mass of the population.

Our reason for considering Mahboub Alhaq's experience in some detail at this point is not so much because his book tells of one thinker's struggle to come to terms with the problems of growth and development as the fact that it represents the unfolding of a major trend in the theory of development. If we refer to *The Poverty Curtain* from time to time, it is because, unlike the great majority of works in development literature, it is based on hard experience rather than on a view from an ivory tower.

At the beginning of his professional life, after graduating from Western universities, Mahboub Alhaq had a blind faith in the philosophy of growth.

> We have to accept that economic growth is a process which is not without cruelty and depression. The essence of economic growth is to get the worker to produce more than he is allowed to consume to satisfy his most immediate needs. It is this 'surplus' which is the important thing, call it what we may: 'surplus value', as Marx generally did; 'savings' or 'capital formation' in the terminology of modern economic analysis; or 'the comrades' voluntary contribution

to national growth', as it is called by those who defend communist regimes in their custom of appropriating this surplus.[1]

Mahboub Alhaq's faith was such that he feared the vitality of growth would be sapped by the notions of social justice flowing from the West to the Third World.

> In their policies, the developed countries tend to emphasize such notions as 'wealth distribution' and the creation of a 'welfare state'. This makes sense when individual income reaches a level at which there is a margin for savings and economic institutions have developed to an extent which permits such margins to be exploited . . . It would, however, be unfortunate for us if, whether consciously or unconsciously, we were to borrow these notions from the developed countries and to allow them to influence the philosophy of growth in the Third World.[2]

Following his period of unquestioning faith in growth, Mahboub Alhaq began to see things differently when he was confronted with disquieting and pressing questions. He observed:

> We know that a number of underdeveloped countries have been able to achieve relatively high rates of growth within short periods of time. However, has this growth done anything to alleviate such scourges of poverty as malnutrition, disease, illiteracy and the continuing plight of those with no homes or housing unfit for human habitation? Has this growth led to more opportunities for work or greater equality of opportunity? Has the nature of development kept pace with the hopes and aspirations of the masses?[3]

The reply to each of these questions was in the negative. The answers brought Mahboub Alhaq to the final stage of his intellectual quest and to a destination radically different from its starting-point:

> The goal of development has to be a determined assault on the worst forms of poverty. Development must aim at the gradual elimination of malnutrition, disease, illiteracy, unemployment and the lack of equal opportunity. We used to be taught that we had to confine our attention to GNP and that this would solve the problem of poverty. Now, however, what we need to do is just the opposite: we have to focus our attention on poverty. It is this which will guarantee the solution to the problem of GNP.[4]

The reason for this radical change in Alhaq's viewpoint was his personal experience of rapid growth in Pakistan and his analysis of the economic, political and social results of this growth. They included the concentration of income and wealth from manufacturing in the hands of 22 family corporations. This small number of firms gained control of two-thirds of industry, 80 per cent of banking and 70 per cent of insurance. Meanwhile, the income gap between East and West Pakistan widened and the real wages of industrial workers fell by a third.[5] In short, it was apparent that growth benefited only the fortunate few while the majority gained nothing.

Pakistan, of course, is not the only country to have suffered the effects of rapid growth. In many areas of the Third World the same sombre picture has emerged. In the Arab world, for example, Galal Amin, the Egyptian economist, has shown that only the 'outer crust' was affected by development, while the overwhelming bulk of the population saw no improvement in their situation. Amin's conclusion was that Arab governments were concerned not with development but with modernization. In a biting and honest critique, he said that their efforts had achieved nothing but 'the modernization of poverty'.[6]

Even in a country like Brazil, which every observer would concede has achieved an economic miracle, the growth experience had its full share of horror stories. For example, at a time when incomes in general were rising, the share of the majority in the national income actually fell. In the years between 1960 and 1970, a wealthy minority, accounting for less than 5 per cent of the population, was able to increase its share of national income from 24.7 to 36.6 per cent. During the same period, the share of the overwhelming majority of the population (80 per cent) fell from 45.5 to 37.8 per cent, while that of the other 15 per cent, i.e. those with relatively high incomes, remained steady at around 27 per cent.[7]

The recurrence of this phenomenon in one country after another is such that it might almost be taken as the distinguishing feature of growth in the Third World. Wherever growth had once evoked admiration, its consequences gave rise to dismay and disappointment. Although per capita income throughout the Third World increased at no less than 3 per cent per annum between 1950 and 1970, this rate of growth did not bring sufficient employment opportunities to provide work for a large and expanding labour force, and the benefits were not passed on to the broad mass of the population with low incomes.[8]

Indeed, according to the findings of some researchers, three decades of development have resulted in greater inequality in many countries of the Third World, while the situation of most of the people has not improved at all. Meanwhile, poverty has worsened in poor, overpopulated countries. It would appear, then, that there is substance in the saying: 'With development, the rich get richer and the poor get poorer.'

So, who has benefited from development efforts in the Third World? The main beneficiary everywhere is the ruling élite and that section of society which has battened on to it. This is true whether the élite is a military junta, a parliamentary party or a traditional conservative system of government. It does not take a lot of thought to realize that no ruling élite will initiate development changes which would threaten its own survival. And if such a decision is taken, it will not last for long. We have only to look at what happened in Peru in 1968 and in Ghana in 1971 when the government decided to devalue the currency. Both regimes fell immediately because the decision damaged the interests of a ruling class consisting of military men and bureaucrats.[10]

In a classical analysis of bureaucracy, Anthony Down found that bureaucratic behaviour has four main traits.[11] Consider each one of these in turn and see how they translate into the practical realities of development:

First, the bureaucrat tends to alter the information which he passes on to his superior by exaggerating the importance of that which is of benefit to him and by minimizing the importance of that which is not.

Translated into practice, this means that if a bureaucrat was asked to gather information which would assist in taking a decision on the location of, say, an electricity project, he might manipulate statistics in the hope that this might lead to the project being switched to his preferred region.[12]

Secondly, every official is naturally biased in favour of policies and actions which serve his interests and is opposed to policies which conflict with his interests.

Translated into practice, this means that if a bureaucrat was asked to study a new tax which might affect the bureaucrat himself, he would probably find a hundred and one reasons to strangle the proposed tax at birth. But if the same bureaucrat was asked to carry out a feasibility study for the creation of a new credit institution, whose services he might find personally beneficial, he would highlight the advantages.

Thirdly, the speed with which an official responds to the instructions issued to him would depend on whether they suit his interests.

Translated into practice, this means that if an instruction was issued for a department to be relocated from a small town with few amenities to a larger and more attractive one, the departmental staff would carry out the order with lightning speed. However, if the order was for the relocation of the department from a town to a village in the middle of nowhere, it would go straight into the drawer and stay there with not the slightest chance of seeing the light of day.

Fourthly, the extent to which a bureaucrat will seek new responsibilities and agree to take risks depends on the degree to which such new responsibilities help him to further his personal interests.

Translated into practice, this means that a civil servant in a department which deals directly with the public, such as a director of customs, telephone services or education, has a considerable social standing and, with a modicum of effort, can achieve promotion. However, if such promotion would relegate him to a quiet office and deny him the social standing he enjoys, the additional effort would never be made. On the other hand, if the new post carried a high social profile, the additional effort would be forthcoming immediately.[13]

This is how the wheels of bureaucracy turn and, with them, the wheels of development.

Now, if this is the case with a bureaucracy which does not readily take bribes or give in to corruption, what of a bureaucracy which is both corrupt and corrupting? While there is no doubt that a venal bureaucracy is capable of great harm wherever it may be found, the danger is all the more serious in the poor countries of the Third World. Realistic and accurate figures which would give a true picture of the effects of administrative corruption are difficult if not impossible to come by. Hardly surprising, as corrupt officials do not usually advertise their 'achievements'. Nevertheless, there is sufficient information about corruption to give an idea of its terrible effects.

In one of the few studies of its kind, Gould and Amaro-Reyes provide vivid insights into the havoc wreaked by administrative corruption in the Third World. They found that 75 per cent of the members of parliament in Thailand received commissions and bribes and that the cost of corruption to the country was around US$800 million per annum, i.e. approximately 50 per cent of the State budget.[14] A study carried out in 1980 found that, in Zaire, about two-thirds of those registered as State employees were just names and did not exist. The salaries paid to these ghost employees in 1978 amounted to 288 million zaires, i.e. the equivalent of half the budget deficit for that year.[15] Another study carried out in Mexico reported that corruption follows the citizen, quite literally, from the cradle to the grave: to get a birth certificate, you need to pay a bribe and to get a death certificate you need to pay another.[16]

The study concludes that the data and statistics available indicate that the bureaucratic institutions in most Third World countries have become power centres which obey no one and are responsible to no one. They work towards their own goals through organized extortion and corruption and their tentacles spread everywhere, helped by the already huge and ever-increasing number of bureaucratic regulations.[17] The study comes to the following conclusion:

> Corruption flourishes in the countries of Asia, Africa and Latin America. A State monopoly over economic activities, political immaturity, widespread poverty, an absence of social and economic justice, administrative incompetence and the fact that people do not recognize the legitimacy of the existing government have all contributed to creating a fertile soil for corruption, with deadly effects on the efficiency of the administration and on the political and social development of the country.[18]

A vivid account of everyday corruption in a Third World country involving an ordinary man in the street trying to pay his telephone bill, is provided by an Arab journalist as follows:

> In the first place, the subscriber must appear in person to obtain the bill, which, no doubt, dates back to the days of Turkish rule when the bankrupt aga roamed the streets crying at the top of his voice, 'Alms! I am your master.' Getting the bill, however, is just the beginning! When it comes to pay, God help the miserable subscriber. He must then stand in the queue for hours on end. Unless, of course, he is smart and has the money. If this is case, he will find a contact in the administration, someone 'in the know' to speed up the payment process. Failing this, he has no choice but to pay a bribe to settle his bill . . . Just imagine it! He has to pay a bribe so that the authority will be good enough to let him pay his bills.[19]

And what happens to the hapless man in the street when the time comes for him to renew his car licence every year?

> First, there is the meeting with the test inspector and, of course, the test always discovers faults. Sometimes because they actually exist, sometimes because, as everyone knows, the inspector, like the beggar, feels he is entitled to his due. Once this hurdle has been cleared, our friend faces a new obstacle: he has to obtain a certificate to show that he has paid any outstanding traffic fines, with any luck managing to get a reduction on the inflated figures shown on his sheet. Only then can he go to the insurance company. If providence smiles on him there, he must next proceed post haste to the cashier and pay his tax. However, unless he gets there before a quarter to twelve, he will hear the fatal words 'Would you kindly come back tomorrow, sir?[20]

If the honest citizen has to face such difficulties in trying to pay a phone bill or a car tax due to the State, one can only wonder what a gauntlet he will have to run in order to obtain what is due to him. These observations apply to virtually all the Third World countries.

In this context, I am reminded of a management consultant from an Asian country who came to Saudi Arabia at the end of the 1960s to study the customs procedures applying in the Kingdom, with the aim of simplifying and streamlining them. After spending some time examining the procedures, he announced that he was astonished to find how simple they were and that he would try to apply them in his own country.[21]

Can anyone blame the late Jawaharlal Nehru for telling fellow leaders of the Third World at the Bandung Conference in 1955, when development fever was at its peak: 'I fear that we shall find the fate of development in the hands of corrupt bureaucracies in some countries and incompetent ones in others.'[22] And could anyone blame us now in 1994 for adding: 'And in many of them, both'?

After the ruling élite and the bureaucracy, the next in line at the development trough are the inhabitants of the capitals and cities. The great majority of projects in health, education, housing and communications are carried out in the major cities, while the villages and rural areas are left on the sidelines and their inhabitants are denied all public services.

To illustrate the privileged position of capital cities, let us take Tehran during the mid-1970s as an example. At that time, the city had one-third of all State employees, 60 per cent of the student population and approximately 50 per cent of all doctors (i.e. half of Iran's doctors were treating just 10 per cent of the population). In Tehran, one person in ten owned a car, whereas, in the country as a whole, the figure was one in ninety. Some 820,000 copies of daily newspapers were printed for the capital but only some 25,000 copies for the provinces. In short, the opportunities open to the residents of the capital for education and civil service work and the amenities and services available to them were far greater than those enjoyed by anyone in the provinces.[23] The story of Tehran can be repeated for every Third World capital.

Yet, in the end, the advantages enjoyed by Tehran led to its downfall. From the villages and countryside of Iran, people flocked in millions to the capital in search of work and shelter. But the bounty of the city did not reach down to the newcomers. All too soon they found themselves living without work in wretched conditions, while there, before their very eyes, lay obscene wealth, not one crumb of which fell their way. To whom could these 'peasants of the capital' turn for comfort in their suffering, their sense of exile, their yearning for family and friends? To no one but to the man of religion. Present at every birth, every marriage, every divorce and every death, he was as close to them in the drudgery and woes of their everyday life as the power of the Shah was utterly remote from their hopes and expectations. When the men of religion called on these peasants of the capital to rise they did so at once and followed them. Those who have nothing are easily mobilized to sweep away those who have everything.

Following the fall of the Shah in 1976, it was assumed in the West that his downfall was due to his eagerness to develop Iran; that, paradoxically, development bred revolution. The first to adopt this line of reasoning was Henry Kissinger and many others followed in his train. Yet, the facts suggest that the opposite was the case. The collapse of the Iranian regime came about because development failed, not because it succeeded. Were it not for the fact that Iran's development plans failed miserably – a failure due as much to the philosophy of development as to incompetence in implementation[24] – millions of people would not have uprooted themselves from their villages and farms and turned the capital into a human time-bomb. The

Iranian revolution still rings warning bells for the leaders of the Third World and its moral is: 'If you want stability, transform the countryside into the capital and not vice versa.'

It should be noted that, after the fall of the Shah, many predicted that what had happened in Iran would be repeated in the Arab States of the Gulf. However, there are fundamental differences between the internal situation in Iran under the Shah and that of the Gulf States. In this context, the most relevant of these differences is the emergence of a middle class in the Gulf with an interest in maintaining the stability of the regime. Here, as elsewhere, the middle class is the prerequisite for stability and the fate of stability everywhere is linked to the fate of this class. Thus, it can be said that political stability in the Gulf is intimately linked with the future of the middle class. This stability would be put at risk if the middle classes were out-weighed by the poor.

We can now assert that we must develop in the interests of the vast majority of the people. To do so, it is necessary, first, to prevent the fruits of development from being monopolized by the ruling élite; second, to put an end to the monopoly of privilege enjoyed by the inhabitants of the capital; and, third, to rescue development from the claws of bureaucracy and corruption. But this alone is not enough. Development must be protected against a disease which is no less dangerous than administrative corruption, namely inflation.

It is beyond the scope of this little book to discuss in detail the concept of inflation and its causes, whether structural or cyclical. Much has been written on this subject. Suffice it to say that inflation means a fall in the purchasing power of money (due to an increase in the price of goods and services) and a concomitant fall in the standard of living of the citizens. Hyperinflation turns life into a nightmare.[25]

A friend who used to live in Eastern Europe before the collapse of the Communist regimes, told me how hyperinflation reduced the value of paper money to nothing, and the only recognized currency was American cigarettes. All kinds of goods and services were bought and sold using this means of exchange: a handful of cigarettes would buy a chicken, while a few cartons would pay for the services of the best doctors.

If development is to serve the great majority of the people, we will have to turn away once and for all from the idea of spontaneous 'growth' and to focus all our efforts on guided 'development', the first goal of which must be to put an end to poverty.[26] This view first came on to the stage during the 1970s and then began to gain currency in the 1980s. However, most development plans in the Third World still follow the same old pattern.

The new doctrine requires, among other things, a three-pronged approach. In the first place, the production and consumption of goods must be measured in terms of the public interest, and equitable distribution must be given the same importance as sufficiency of production. Secondly, a clear strategy must be drawn up to wage war on poverty, with policies aimed at eliminating excessive differences in income and standards of living, whether between individuals, groups or regions. Last but not least, political decision-making must be developed in such a way as to ensure greater popular participation. Thus, economic decisions will reflect the needs and priorities of the various forces within society.[27]

The strategy to combat poverty must consist of policies designed to involve the poor in the economy of the country by providing employment opportunities rather than increasing social security; to raise the productivity of small farmers and agricultural workers;[28] to reform existing institutions, such as banks, schools and public amenities, so that the services they provide are made available to lower income groups as well as to the rich.[29]

This approach, however, cannot be adopted by means of a simple ministerial decision, instructions from a ministry official, a sub-plan or an interim policy. It has to come from the very highest levels.

> This direct assault on mass poverty is essentially a decision for politicians rather than technocrats. Unless the decision is taken at the very highest political level and unless all the political forces in the country are mobilized to defend and implement it, any plan drawn up will remain nothing more than a theoretical exercise.[30]

Yet, as the present lines are being written, the Third World is on the verge of transforming its Ministries of Planning into 'Centres for Theoretical Exercises'.

NOTES

1 Mahboub Alhaq, *The Poverty Curtain*, New York, Columbia University Press, 1976, p. 3.

2 Ibid., p. 5.

3 Ibid., p. 31.

4 Ibid., p. 35.

5 Ibid., p. 6.

6 Galal Amin, *The Modernization of Poverty*, Leiden, E. J. Brill, 1974, p. 110.

7 See Ozay Mehemet, *Economic Planning and Social Justice in Developing Countries*, New York, St Martin's Press, 1978, p. 51.

8 See Paul Streeten *et al.*, *First Things First*, published for the World Bank by Oxford University Press, 1981, p. 11.

9 Malcolm Gillis *et al.*, *Economics of Development*, New York, W. W. Norton & Co., 1983, p. 70.

10 Ibid., p. 25.

11 Anthony Down, *Inside Bureaucracy*, Boston, Mass., Little, Brown & Co., 1967, p. 266.

12 Exaggerating the size of the population is a well-known way of obtaining a project. When the author was in charge of electricity in the Kingdom of Saudi Arabia, he would often meet village leaders who would ask for an electricity project for their village and they would never forget to multiply the population several times over. He very quickly became accustomed to dividing the figures given by five or even ten to arrive at the true figure.

13 Sometimes, the only way an official can be moved is to 'kick him upstairs'. The only difference is that, whereas in the West he would

be made chairman of the board, in the Third World, he is usually promoted to the post of adviser.

14 David J. Gould and José A. Amaro-Reyes, *The Effects of Corruption on Administrative Performance: Illustrations from Developing Countries*, World Bank, Staff Working Papers, No. 580, 1983, p. 8.

15 Ibid., p. 10.

16 Ibid., p. 16.

17 Ibid., p. 33.

18 Ibid., p. 33.

19 Mahmoud al-Saadani, *al-Musawwir*, 2 (Feb. 1990), p. 82.

20 Ibid., p. 82.

21 Afterwards, when the task was assigned to some young Saudi researchers from the Institute of Public Administration in Riyadh, they succeeded so well in getting rid of complicated time-consuming procedures that the customs system of the Kingdom has become a model of its kind.

22 Muhammad Hasanain Haikal, *History Revisited*, Beirut, All Prints Distribution & Publishing Co., 1985, p.269.

23 Robert Graham, *Iran: The Illusion of Power*, London, Croom Helm, 1978, p. 28. The remarkable thing about this book is that it was written while the Shah was still in power, unlike so many others published after his overthrow, filled with the wisdom of hindsight.

24 The basic aim of development was not, as the Shah declared, connected with the living standards of Iranians but with making Iran the fifth strongest military power in the world.

25 When inflation peaked in Germany during the 1920s, it took millions of marks loaded into a car to buy a single loaf of bread.

26 Getting rid of abject poverty is not an impossibility. It is said of the period of Umar bin Abdulaziz: 'Umar in his lifetime made the man bring us great wealth and ask us to give it to the poor. No one would take it but Umar made the people rich.' See al-Suyuti, *History of the Caliphs*, Cairo, al-Maktaba al-Tijariyya al-Kubra, 1952, p. 235.

27   See Mehemet, op. cit., p. 177.

28   Mahboub Alhaq, op. cit., p. 22.

29   Ibid., p. 61.

30   Ibid., p. 64.

CHAPTER 3

What Do
We Develop?

Let them adore the Lord
Of this House,
Who provides them
With food against hunger,
And with security
Against fear.

The Qur'an

What Do
We Develop?

What do we develop? The era of random growth came to a close, in historical terms, at the end of the 1940s, when it was replaced by planned development. According to the planners, development could succeed only if new values were 'implanted' into traditional societies. Thus, Marxists held that for development to take place, it was necessary to remove the old ruling class and its outmoded ideas and to replace it by a new class with new (Marxist) ideas. Capitalists, on the other hand, held that the Third World could not develop unless old traditions and customs were removed and replaced by new (capitalist) customs and traditions.

Although W. W. Rostow, the famous American economist, called his theory 'A Non-Communist Manifesto for Development',[1] the difference between his proposed stages for development and those of the Marxists was much smaller than he at the time or his disciples and supporters later imagined. In the mind of Rostow, and in the mind of the Marxists, a backward society fettered by old traditions and outmoded customs would come to a stage at which it would 'open up' to the progressive ideas which would free it from the shackles of tradition and custom. Rostow saw these progressive ideas as being those of capitalism while the Marxists saw them as being those of socialism. The next stage would be 'take-off', when the ties of tradition and custom would fall away, leaving society ready to soar away towards the heavens of Rostow's capitalism or the Marxists' socialism. A fourth stage of economic growth would then be followed by a fifth stage of maturity. Again, Rostow saw all this as coming about through the capitalist model while the socialists saw it in terms of the Marxist model.

It is surprising that the intellectual foundations of development economics were not developed in the Third World. Though the roll-call of illustrious names in development literature runs into hundreds, the number of non-Westerners among them could be counted on the fingers of one hand. Not a single thinker from the Third World has won a Nobel prize for development economics. Not a single African or Asian scholar has managed to develop a comprehensive or quasi-comprehensive theory of development. Most Third World theorists have been the star pupils of First and Second World masters.

Thus development fell prey to a cultural invasion. Development planners in the Third World believed that the first thing which needed to be developed was an imported mentality, whether such a mentality was brought in from the capitalist West or from the socialist East. In other words, the importation of ideas became an end instead of a means. The disciples of the West came to preach liberal theories to the poor and illiterate populations of Third World. To the same audience, the disciples of the East came bearing the works of Karl Marx and glad tidings of education and an end to poverty. While the masses of the Third World looked on, the intellectuals fought out their battles in a struggle which was sometimes amicable, sometimes bloody. Governments came and went. Coups were mounted here and revolutions broke out there. As one philosophy waxed, another waned. And all the while, the plight of the poor remained unchanged.

The ideas imported from the capitalist and the socialist worlds agreed on one point: industry was the key to development in the Third World. Capitalism arrived at this conclusion for historical reasons connected with the birth of the Industrial Revolution in Europe and the resulting emergence of an industrialized society with industrial, capitalist values. Marxism came to the same conclusion on ideological grounds: the essence of the theory, in the days before Lenin, was that socialism could not be achieved from the basis of a backward, feudal, agricultural economy but only by way of industrialization.

Thus the ruling élites of the Third World had no option but to industrialize. Plans for development were plans for industrialization. Efforts to obtain finance generally looked for money for industrial projects. The iron and steel complex became the badge of development which no Third World country could forgo, an image to display on its postage stamps, the destination for visitors, the subject for essays in countless schools. The new technocrats were now the rising élite of society, whether, under capitalist systems, where they owned the plants themselves or whether, under socialist systems, where they controlled them in the name of the State. Meanwhile, industrial workers as a class were rapidly becoming superior to their fellow workers in agriculture.

And, everywhere, industry was the focus of a wide-ranging debate. It would be argued that the aim of industrialization must be autarky or the minimizing of imports. In some quarters it would be said that the aim must be to export. In others it was believed that self-sufficiency should come to industries in which the State enjoyed some distinct advantage. Elsewhere it would be contended that industrialization was possible even in the absence of such an advantage. While some argued for heavy industry, others argued the case for light industry. While some pleaded the advantages of high technology, others propounded the benefits of labour-intensive projects. While some opted for giant industrial complexes, others maintained that cottage industry was the right course, i.e. a system of domestic or quasi-domestic units usually operated by the members of a single household.

However, the whole debate over Third World industrialization, at that time and even now, focused on detail rather than the main issue. No one ever questioned the principle that industrialization was the key to development.

The notion of industrialization seemed all the more attractive because of the achievements of the Soviet Union during the inter-war and postwar periods. The world stood back in amazement at the sight of an agricultural country – in many respects a backward one – rapidly transforming itself, first into an industrialized State and then into a superpower alongside the USA. We need not concern ourselves here with the fact that the picture just sketched is a good deal rosier than the reality – as everyone now knows. Nor is this the place to discuss the human cost paid by the Soviet Union, which was considerable.[2] The important thing is that, from the perspective of the Third World, the experience of the Soviet Union heightened the magical appeal of industrialization and won over hearts and minds everywhere.

If all this borrowing from East and West had only remained within the bounds of industrialization, it might yet have been harmless. After all, was it not industrialization which enabled the countries of the First World to transform relatively cheap raw materials into high-value manufactured products? Is it not industrialization which is the ideal way to transfer technology?[3] Is it not industrialization which has enabled a number of Third World countries to make their way into the club of developed States, notably those that development literature refers to as 'the

Gang of Four', i.e. South Korea, Nationalist China, Hong Kong and Singapore. However, the problem is that the process did not stop with industrialization. Instead, development became an attempt to adopt everything foreign and to smother at birth everything home-grown.

Development sought not so much to improve the economic, social and political conditions of the citizen as to change his identity and undermine his sense of belonging. In the end, like the crow in the fable, it succumbed to temptation and abandoned its old way of walking without learning how to walk in the new way. Though the attempt to obliterate old identities reached a climax with Atatürk, yet, in many parts of the Third World, that example has inspired lesser Atatürks to follow in his footsteps.[4]

The ruling élites were infatuated with the West and divorced from the beliefs and values cherished by their own society. In their attitudes and lifestyle, they were closer to those who lived in the capitals of the West than to the masses it was their duty to govern.

Inevitably, therefore, development was the reflection of the achievements of the First World. But the reflection was seen through the glass of a distorting mirror. Constitutions were shipped in lock, stock and barrel from France and Belgium (and, of course, were not long-lived). Laws were brought over wholesale from the Anglo-Saxon countries. Schools teaching in foreign languages appeared everywhere. The height of progress was to spurn national dress and to avoid, wherever possible, speaking the national language. Indians, Arabs and Koreans went to study the philosophy of development at Harvard and Oxford. Cultural authenticity was seen as reactionary and cultural identity as constricting. Even the ideas of liberation which led the countries of the Third World to independence sprang not from their own heritage but from the universities of the colonial powers and the theories of its intellectuals.

Out went the turban and in came the hat. Out went the long robe and in came trousers. Out went the veil and in came the miniskirt. Public institutions and places soon began to echo names from far across the sea: the Sporting Club, the American Hospital, the International School, Spinney's Supermarket, Marine Drive. In came the symbols of the modern age: the hamburger, pizza, Coca-Cola and ketchup. Even the humble red pepper which grows throughout the Third World disappeared from the shelf, to be replaced by Tabasco, imported from the southern states of the USA at twenty times the price of the local product.

Development was a hit-and-miss business of frantic importation, with no vision, no overview, no clear objectives. The inevitable result was, as we have seen, growth of an abnormal kind which benefited a minority and left the overwhelming majority exactly where they were.

Out of the analysis of the results of this blind development, however, there gradually emerged a new philosophy which called for development to be placed at the service of the people rather than for the people to be subjugated in the service of development. The new philosophy of development emerged in the 1980s, arising from the ashes of the old theory of growth which had prevailed since the 1940s. The manner in which this came about has been summarized by a well-known economist, Paul Streeten, as follows:

1. People stopped believing that rapid economic growth was sufficient to achieve development goals and came to the conclusion that such growth was, in general, inadequate. The development of the cultural and social aspects had to keep pace with economic development, even though separate from it. In other words, growth was as much a result as a cause of development.
2. Relying on capital as the sole engine of development ceased and it was realized that it was extremely important to create

the right conditions for development, whether economic, social or cultural.

3. People stopped believing that growth had to come first and that a just distribution of wealth would follow. They came to feel that countries which developed rapidly did not necessarily achieve a just distribution of wealth.

4. Whereas it had been expected that in the development field, the poor countries would follow the same path as that taken by the rich countries, it was now realized that the relationship between the countries of the Third World and the developed world could not be so easily simplified and that the complexities and variables of the relationship might prove an obstacle rather than an aid to development.

5. People lost their absolute faith in industrialization as the most important factor in development and began to see the problems which it brought about. They started to see the importance of developing the agricultural sector – especially small farms – and improving the conditions of those who lived and worked on the farms.

6. The search for the 'best' technology was abandoned in favour of that which was 'most appropriate', i.e. a technology which helps to improve production and distribution without exhausting scarce resources such as skills and capital.

7. People stopped insisting on policies of either exports or self-sufficiency and abandoned sterile discussions of this and that position. Instead, they followed development strategies which took a more flexible form and policies which were more responsive to the realities of time and place.

8. There was no longer insistence on pricing systems, the radical redistribution of wealth or technological development as separate and independent ways of putting an end to the problem of poverty. Instead, it was realized that the adoption of one means to the exclusion of others was useless and

might be harmful and that what was needed was a mix of various means required by the circumstances.

9. People stopped believing that the problem of overpopulation would be solved automatically by growth. Instead, they came to realize that overpopulation is a highly complex problem which cannot be solved by growth alone.[5]

One of the signs of maturity which has begun to pervade development philosophy is an impartial attitude towards traditions, customs and habits rather than the earlier stance of extreme hostility. According to the old theory, tradition in any society represented an obstacle to development and had to be abandoned. The new theory, on the other hand, takes an objective analytical approach, realizing that, while some traditions do impede the process, there are others which are not in conflict with development. On the contrary, they may even help to advance the cause of progress.[6] In this regard, Galal Amin has pointed out that although a society may be religious, follow the extended family model or not give women their full rights, this does not necessarily constitute an obstacle to economic development.[7]

After this brief excursion through half a century of development philosophy, we can now return to our original question: what do we develop? It can be said without equivocation that we must not confine development to a single sector, whether agriculture or industry; to a single service, whether banking or tourism; or to a single set of infrastructure projects, whether roads or electricity. What we have to do is develop all sectors, services and projects which satisfy the basic needs of society. These include not only material needs such as housing, food, work, health, education, sanitation and communications but also security, dignity and freedom.[8]

This new approach, referred to in the UN literature as 'human development',[9] aims to reconcile the production and distribution of goods with the liberation and enrichment of human potential. The approach focuses attention on choice: what can people have and what can people do to enable them to achieve a standard of living in keeping with human dignity? This approach concentrates as much on satisfying basic needs as on developing the person *per se*.[10]

Helping the poor is a noble goal to which we are exhorted by every religion, philosophy and moral principle. Here, however, we are not suggesting that help for the poor is a simple matter of moral choice to be left to the conscience of the individual. On the contrary, we posit it as a basis for development if not the basis. There is, of course, nothing new in saying that meeting the basic needs of the citizen is the best moral choice. What is new is that it is the best choice in economic, political and social terms as well. Thus, even in purely economic terms, channelling investment into satisfying basic needs will often produce greater returns than any other form of investment.[11]

However, acceptance of the theory of 'meeting basic needs' or the theory of 'human development' solves only half the problem, even at the theoretical level. The other more important half of the problem will remain without a solution unless the theory of basic needs is translated into specific programmes of action and expenditure. Development has not the slightest chance of success unless the general aims are first translated into policies. It is a matter of the utmost regret that no ready-made programme exists which can be used in any country of the Third World. All the ready-made models have met with abject failure because they did not take into account the major differences between the countries concerned.

Some experts in this field take the view that, for development purposes, distinctions must be made between different categories of countries: (a) between countries which enjoy a tradition of education and are governed by an educated élite and those where illiteracy is endemic; (b) between countries with developed systems of locally managed trade, finance and communications and those in which such systems are either lacking or are under foreign control; (c) between countries with a population united by language, culture and national identity and those in which such homogeneity is absent; and (d) between countries with a tradition of self-government and those with no history of self-government.[12]

Moreover, it seems plain that development in an Islamic society will differ from development in a Christian, Hindu or Buddhist society. Development in a tribal society will differ from development in a country with no tradition of tribalism. Development in a society of pastoral nomads will differ from development in a society of farmers. When a writer once remarked that 'there are as many development problems as there are developing countries', this was no exaggeration but a faithful reflection of the facts.

With these obvious differences, it is quite clear that what is perceived as a basic requirement in Country A may be seen as subsidiary in Country B. Similarly, traditions which would allow a requirement to be achieved in Country C might stand in the way of its achievement in Country D. Moreover, the problem is not limited to differences between countries. Even within a single country, basic needs may vary from one region to another, depending on geography, climate and human character.[13]

So, where do we go from here? How can we translate the philosophy of development into clear aims and objectives, into policies and programmes? How can we tackle the divergences which make the problems of one society different from those of another in terms of the root causes, implications and the means to solve them? The answer to all of these questions is: planning. Planning is the indispensable preliminary.

NOTES

1 W. W. Rostow, *Politics and the Stages of Growth*, Cambridge, Cambridge University Press, 1971.

2 It is now clear that the roots of the economic collapse presently being experienced by the former Soviet Union lie in ideology and a misdirected industrialization which concentrated on the military sector at the expense of all others. However, what is so obvious with the benefit of hindsight was not at all apparent before the 1980s.

3 For the positive effects of industrialization and its role in development, see Ghazi Abdulrahman Algosaibi, *Face to Face with Development*, 2nd edn, Jeddah, Tihama, AH1410/AD1989.

4 One sign of greater maturity in the field of development economics is the fact that Atatürk has lost much of the status he once enjoyed in the Third World and among its ruling élites. I myself was once involved in a minor diplomatic crisis for refusing to visit the tomb of Atatürk as part of the programme scheduled for me on an official visit to Turkey. I believed then – as I do now – that it would be the height of hypocrisy for a Muslim to visit the burial place of someone who displayed an unparalleled hostility to Islam.

5 Sanjaya Lall and Frances Stewart, *Theory and Reality in Development*, New York, St Martin's Press, 1986, pp. 21–2.

6 See Nath Varma Baiydia, *The Sociology and Politics of Development: A Theoretical Study*, London, Routledge & Kegan Paul, 1980, p. 10.

7 See Galal Amin, *The Modernization of Poverty*, Leiden, E. J. Brill, 1974, p. 110.

8 Proof of the importance of non-material needs is the fact that the demise of the communist regimes was due as much to their inability to satisfy people's instinctive needs for freedom, dignity and private

ownership and their right to be treated as individual human beings rather than just numbers, as to the inability of the regimes to satisfy their material needs.

9 United Nations literature sees 'human development' as a theory separate from the earlier theory of meeting basic needs. My own view is that a basic needs theory which takes into account non-material needs is practically the same as a 'human development' theory. For this reason, I have treated the two concepts as being synonymous.

10 See *UN Human Development Report for 1990*, New York, Oxford University Press, 1990, p. 11.

11 Paul Streeten *et al.*, *First Things First: Meeting Basic Human Needs in Developing Countries*, London, Oxford University Press, 1981, p. 111.

12 See Malcolm Gillis *et al.*, *Economics of Development*, New York, W. W. Norton & Co., 1983, p. 18.

13 In the kingdom of Saudi Arabia, for example, when the government began to open girls' schools during the early 1960s, there was fierce opposition in some regions and security forces had to be sent in to protect the schools from the wrath of families protesting against them. However, after a few years, the same regions began to ask for more girls' schools. Education for girls was no longer rejected out of hand but was perceived as a basic need. This change within a relatively short space of time was the result of a change in popular perception.

CHAPTER 4

How Do
We Develop?

(Joseph) said: 'For seven years
Shall ye diligently sow
As is your wont:
And the harvests that ye reap,
Ye shall leave them in the ear,
Except a little, of which
Ye shall eat.'
                    The Qur'an

How Do
We Develop?

Planning is not an intellectual luxury or a decorative touch to make the development process more attractive to the eye of the beholder. Planning does not mean reports written in a vacuum and destined for the wastepaper basket. It should not offer bureaucrats the chance to bask in their splendid buildings and highflown titles, nor does it mean the wholesale production of recommendations by home-grown or foreign consultancies. What planning does mean is intelligent effort directed on a daily basis to the realities on the ground and to the aspirations of its people; the kind of effort which seeks to bring these aspirations in line with these realities, while at the same time, developing them as much as possible to meet the people's aspirations. The more points of contact there are between the aspirations and the reality, the more likely planning will succeed.

It may be helpful at this point to review the long history of planning in the Third World in order to examine the results and to see what lessons can be learned. Planning began in earnest after the Second World War which was no coincidence since the warring countries had been in need of careful planning in various fields so that they could concentrate their military efforts and put the available resources to the best possible use. The success achieved through planning during the war was the main reason for its widespread use in later years. Moreover, in many countries of the Third World, there was a general belief that the successes of the Soviet Union were primarily due to its series of Five-Year Plans. In addition the fact that many of the countries of the Third World are centrally controlled made it easy to subject their economies to planning. For these reasons, we can understand why planning has flourished during the second half of the century.

Since 1950, there have been some 300 development plans in the Third World. A field-study of them found that, broadly speaking, they can be divided into three categories:

1. Planning in the 'Soviet belt' including countries in Asia, Eastern Europe and North Africa. The plans were greatly influenced by the Soviet model and socialist ideas. They sought to be as comprehensive and detailed as possible.
2. Planning in the desert regions of Africa, Central Africa and the Caribbean. These plans might be seen as no more than 'symbolic pronouncements', the development process being carried out according to the traditions of the colonial power.
3. Planning in Latin America. The plans here were essentially for industrial development with the primary aim of reducing imports.[1]

How did these plans work in reality? Practical experience has shown that the best performance was not achieved by countries which drew up detailed plans (e.g. India, Bangladesh, Ethiopia and Turkey). Nor was the best performance achieved by countries whose plans were purely symbolic (e.g. Nigeria,

Senegal, Argentina, Ghana, Jamaica and Chile). Success went to those countries which were neither extravagant nor wasteful and were flexible and moderate in their approach to planning (e.g. Korea, Malaysia and Kenya).[2]

Two main lessons can be drawn from these experiences of the Third World. First, the view that a free economy means, among other things, freedom from planning of any kind, proved wrong. The second lesson is that planning cannot succeed if plans are rigid and over-detailed and ignore reality in all its daily variations. Intelligent planning learns as much from real life as it teaches, and strives to change priorities and programmes to meet changes in the real world.[3] If development without planning is fraught with danger, then persisting with a plan which has shown itself to be faulty is, in development terms, foolhardy and irresponsible.

The starting-point for effective, intelligent, flexible planning is the awareness that society consists of systems, which are like molecules in constant interaction with each other rather than separate units which can be dealt with in isolation.[4] If there is one big error in planning which gives rise to all the smaller ones, it is ignorance of the 'laws of systems', that is working with individual parts without taking into account all the others. The 'laws of systems' are all-embracing and, any plan which neglects them is bound to fail in its objectives. Indeed, the end-result may be objectives which differ from and conflict with those which were intended.

However, society is not the only co-ordinated system requiring care and precision in dealing with the whole or with the parts. Nature, too, is a system in which no harm can come to any part without its effects being felt on all the others. I remember hearing the Duke of Edinburgh, speaking as head of the World Wildlife Fund, say that the famines in Africa were the inevitable result of man's disregard for the environment.[5] Prince Philip, however, in his enthusiasm to protect wildlife, sees potential environmental catastrophe in many large-scale projects, such as dams, even though they may be vital in development terms.

Over a decade ago, while on an official visit to Brazil, I came face to face with the Amazon forests, the sheer size of which is unimaginable to anyone who has never seen them with his own eyes. When I asked my host, Brazil's Minister of Planning at the time, why the country was not exploiting this vast natural resource, he answered:

> The best use for these forests is to leave them as they are. The Amazon rain forests are a major source of the world's oxygen. They are the lungs of the planet. Any change in them would lead to an environmental disaster of immeasurable and worldwide consequences.

At the time, I found the answer unconvincing. How was it possible to leave these virgin forests untouched? Now, however, we all believe that the Minister was right. As the forests retreat before the onslaught from man, the dangers to the environment are becoming clear, and the world is beginning to worry about its main source of oxygen. Slowly and somewhat belatedly, international efforts have started to help Brazil to save what remains of the rain forests.

The disruption caused by man to the ecosystem – whether by poisoning rivers, lakes and seas with industrial wastes, by polluting the atmosphere with fumes or by chopping down the forests – can be seen all over the globe. In Western Europe, acid rain falls on the forests and the trees are poisoned where they stand. Acid rain is the distilled product of industrial progress, mankind sending its foul black smoke up into the stratosphere only for it to return eventually in precipitation. Everywhere in the Third World, hunger, which will heed no voice of reason, drives people to destroy the earth on which their future will depend. Acting in good faith to alleviate the pangs of hunger, they may do something as simple as uprooting a tree. This may have dire consequences. In Ethiopia, for example, people cut down the trees for firewood and to make room for cultivation. However, the trees played a vital part in providing protection against the winds and in retaining the soil. With no roots to hold it in place, it was not long before the fertile topsoil had been washed away, turning whole regions into a barren waste. The whole sorry tale of what happened in Ethiopia has been repeated over and over again elsewhere in Africa (Sudan and Somalia), in Latin America (Brazil and Venezuela) and in Asia (Indonesia and Nepal).

Throughout the Third World, poor peasants cut down trees so that they can till the reclaimed land. But their efforts bear fruit for no more than one or two growing seasons. Then, the rains come and remove the topsoil which the trees had shielded, leaving behind bare earth that will support neither trees nor crops. Apart from these direct effects, there are other indirect effects resulting from deforestation and the disruption of the climatic cycles of rain and drought.[6]

If these are the inevitable results of man's tampering with the ecosystem, what are the effects of his interference in the system underlying society? Here again, the effects are devastating.

Perhaps the best way of illustrating my point is to show what it was in a number of Third World countries that disrupted the system underlying society. The first mistake was to neglect the agricultural sector. During the 1950s, Communist China followed the Soviet model by concentrating on industry to the neglect of agriculture. The steep fall in agricultural yields which resulted was so worrying that, by the end of the 1960s and the start of the 1970s, the government had to change its priorities and concentrate investment on agriculture and, especially, on fertilizers.[7] (When the USSR failed to do the same, disaster struck at the end of the 1980s.)

The Chinese experience was repeated in a number of African countries which, during the post-independence years, remained convinced that agriculture needed no attention from the State.[8] The planners in these countries forgot the basic fact that to neglect agriculture means, quite simply, condemning to a life of grinding poverty the vast majority of the population, for whom agriculture is the sole means of livelihood. This attitude towards agriculture in the Third World was changed only under the pressure of famine.

One of the most damaging trends in the Third World is the disruption to the system underlying society by the heavy emphasis placed on military spending at the expense of other sectors. Military expenditure is a bottomless pit, a rapacious devourer of resources which is constantly asking for more. The arms-producing countries sell to the Third World military technology of limited capability and only after the most careful scrutiny. No sooner have the purchasers familiarized themselves with the weapons than they are obsolete, thus creating a need for more sophisticated and more expensive technology. And the cost of sophisticated weaponry is astronomical. In the USA, for example, a single Stealth bomber costs around a billion dollars!

The worst aspect of military expenditure in the poorer countries of the Third World is that it is at the expense of the basic needs of the people. The cost of a single military aircraft is enough to build a number of schools and health centres. Yet, over the last thirty years, the Third World has increased its military spending at three times the rate of the industrialized countries. The Third World's bill for military spending is in excess of two hundred billion dollars per annum. These figures are frightening enough. Even more frightening, however, is the fact that some Third World countries spend between two and four times as much on the military as they do on education and health.[9] For every doctor in the Third World, there are eight soldiers.[10]

Another fatal mistake of Third World planners was to disrupt the system by favouring large cities at the expense of country towns and villages. In 1970, city-dwellers represented 29 per cent of the population of the world; by 1985, this figure had risen to 41 per cent. During the same period, urban populations in the Third World rose from 17 to 31 per cent. Whereas in the developed world emigration to the large cities has been slowing down perceptibly, the Third World continues to see a vast exodus from the villages to the towns, so that, at the end of the century, the majority of the population will be city-dwellers.[11] By that time, the world will have ten super-cities with populations of over 13 million and, of these, eight will be in the Third World and only two outside it.[12]

In Saudi Arabia, ministries responsible for public utilities were put on the spot by a flood of requests to connect mains services to remote villages. A number of attempts were made to plan for population centres to be established as a focus for these small villages and to concentrate services there in order to attract people to settle. However, none of the plans came to anything because the people of the villages kept up their demands until they were eventually connected. The decision to accede to their requests was a political one which was not left to the technocrats. The view of the technocrats was that the money and effort needed to take mains services to a small number of people living in tiny villages in the middle of nowhere would be out of all proportion to the forecast development returns. However, in the light of what has happened in many places in the Third World, where the cities have been swamped by rural populations, the political decision proved wiser than the technocratic one, despite the cost. In this connection, it may be worth pointing out that although technocrats are undoubtedly the best people to carry out development projects, they are not necessarily the best qualified to gauge the mood of the population and to grasp their basic needs.

All of this goes to show that the countries of the Third World are making a big mistake when they assign the task of planning to foreign experts, whether they are individuals, companies or countries. Though the foreign expert may have the required technological information, he will usually lack the feel and familiarity needed to assess the hopes and aspirations of the people. When we say that basic needs are the focus of development, we mean human needs. Thus, knowledge of the people is far more important than any expertise in accounting, economics or engineering.

When I was appointed Minister of Industry and Electricity in 1975, I found that the foreign company responsible for planning a power-station project covering the Al-Qasim region had proposed a 100-megawatt capacity. The company had based its calculation on a doubling of the existing power consumption. What had escaped the notice of the company was that existing demand was low because supply was low; once power became available, there would be an immediate surge in demand. In the face of fierce opposition from 'the experts' – both foreign and national[13] – I insisted that the capacity had to be several times greater than that proposed and I got my way. Once the project had been completed, it became apparent that not even the new capacity was sufficient to meet the increase in demand.

Another gross mistake made by development planners in the Third World is their inability to distinguish between necessities and luxuries. The 'opening up' of the market, which is hailed as an effective way of stimulating the economy and so meeting the basic needs of the people, very often turns into a runaway consumer boom which benefits no one except the manufacturers of the First World.

In this technological age, the presence of a television set in every home in the Third World may be seen as a 'necessity'. However, no one in his right mind would consider it as a 'basic necessity' for the masses. As for multi-system video-recorders, not even the most generous of us would consider them to be a basic necessity (unless we happen to be the manufacturer or a dealer).

No one would dispute that clothing is a necessity. However, the wish to acquire jeans made by a particular American manufacturer is sheer indulgence. No one would dispute that housing is a necessity. However, if a house takes enough steel and concrete to build a mini-fortress, it is a product of architectural arrogance rather than need. Health care is at the top of everyone's priorities. However, building lavish suites in hospitals smacks more of tourism and the hotel business than of medical care. Although some societies – such as the countries of the First World and the Arab Gulf – can afford luxuries as well as basic necessities, the overwhelming majority of countries must require their planners to decide on which they would rather have: a video or a loaf of bread. Too many, alas, would opt for the video and too few for the loaf!

Not far behind the mistake of confusing basic necessities with luxuries comes the error of replacing a basic need, which can be fully satisfied, with one which is newer, more expensive and more prestigious. A friend of mine, who spent many years in Africa, told me that the people of the country in which he used to live had eaten bread made from maize throughout their history. They were perfectly content to cultivate and eat this crop and they needed no outside help. Then, as fate would have it, there emerged one of those inspired leaders who flourish only in the Third World. Travelling the world on official visits, this leader remarked that people elsewhere ate bread made from wheat and thereupon decided that bread made of maize was unsuitable for a nation which had been blessed by begetting an inspired leader like him. He issued the orders to import wheat. The people grew accustomed to the new loaf and the growing of maize soon became a thing of the past. Meanwhile the cost of importing wheat grew to such astronomical proportions that the budget could not meet the bill, and the country was forced to borrow. In the end, the people were without their new wheat loaf, just as they were without their old maize bread.

If development sets its sights on meeting the basic needs of the people, these needs must be understood as they are understood by those who live in the villages and rural areas instead of being determined by planners, the men in suits, sitting in comfortable offices in the capital, surrounded by foreign experts and foreign theories. One of the planning mistakes made in many parts of the Third World was to import exact replicas of the 'match-box' housing of the industrial countries. And, as usual, when the Third World imports from the First World, it imports what had proved to be a failure there. Just when psychologists in the West were coming to the conclusion that the cramped flats found in every Western capital were largely responsible for the depression afflicting those who lived in them, the inspired architects of the Third World adopted the idea and started to build apartment blocks in the heart of the desert.[14]

In Saudi Arabia, for example, it is manifest that the ordinary man in the street would never live in a flat – no matter how comfortable and well-appointed – if he had the means to live in his own house – no matter how primitive. Though this might seem puzzling for an architect or an economist, nothing could be more natural for anyone who really knows the Saudi people. What the Saudi family wants is a reception area for the men and another for the women, each with its own separate entrance and the facilities needed when entertaining guests. It would be difficult to find a flat which could satisfy these requirements.

When the High Dam was built at Aswan in Egypt, local people were rehoused in accommodation built to the very latest design. However, they did not feel at all comfortable in their new houses and longed for the space and freedom of their old homes.[15] Anyone visiting the city of Abu Dhabi will notice camels tethered next to many houses. Keeping a camel in a flat is somewhat difficult to envisage.[16]

We can summarize by saying that development must be directed at satisfying the basic needs of people, whether material or moral. For development to succeed in achieving its goal, the underlying philosophy must be translated into an intelligent, flexible and practical plan, which takes into account and recognizes the 'laws of systems' and practical reality. Perhaps the best way to illustrate the mistakes of development, in theory and practice, is to look at what happened in Iran during the 1970s when the Shah, Muhammad Reza Pahlawi, decided to launch a development campaign which, on paper, was impressive indeed.[17]

Billions of dollars worth of materials and equipment were purchased from the four corners of the earth. Giant freighters from the five continents crossed the seas and queued up outside the ports of Iran. It then dawned on everyone that these old ports were too small for the discharge of the cargoes aboard the waiting fleets. Vessels waited for months on end and demurrage charges rose to more than a billion dollars a year. When the cargoes were finally unloaded, it then emerged that there were no suitable warehouses in or near the ports and the goods were left out in the open at the mercy of the elements. Before long, a large part of the imports, particularly foodstuffs and chemicals, had rotted away. But, as the rest still had to be disposed of, the next step was to move it inland. But there was not enough transport to move the goods and an urgent order had to be placed in Europe for 2,000 trucks. Unfortunately, when they arrived, it turned out that there were not enough Iranians trained to drive them. No time was wasted in importing a large number of Korean drivers. No sooner had they arrived, however, than they realized that they were being paid less than their Iranian counterparts. They promptly went on strike and eventually returned to their homeland. The end-result was that most of the imported equipment and trucks ended on the scrap heap.[18]

All of this might be amusing if it were fiction. Unfortunately, it is a true account of what happened, not just in Iran but in many other places in the Third World. And the same tale continues to be repeated whenever a government decides to develop before doing the necessary planning.[19]

NOTES

1 See Ramgopal Agarwala, *Planning in Developing Countries: Lessons of Experience*, World Bank, Staff Working Papers, No. 516, 1983, p. 5.

2 Ibid., p. 10.

3 During the 1960s, Chile's insistence on sticking to the letter of its plans in the face of changing realities led to many problems. Similarly, there were disastrous results in the development plans of Mexico, Venezuela and Turkey when they tried to proceed with resources which were less than those which had been projected. Ibid., p. 17.

4 An apt description of society as a system is found in a saying by the Prophet Muhammad, in which he compared the society of believers to a single body in which, if one organ suffers from a complaint, the others all respond with sleeplessness or fever.

5 There is no doubt that most of the responsibility for these famines rests with the African regimes concerned, which are an amalgam of ignorance, dictatorship and corruption.

6 I owe this information to field-work carried out by a friend, the Finnish Ambassador Kai Helenuis who saw what was happening for himself when he was in charge of foreign aid at the Economic Section of Finland's Ministry of Foreign Affairs.

7 See Gillis, op. cit., p. 47.

8 It is a paradox that, while the Third World was neglecting agriculture, the First World countries were spending vast amounts on this sector in aid and subsidies, despite the fact that it involves less than 10 per cent of their population. In this context, the Saudi experience in growing wheat has proved beneficial and has produced positive results despite the high cost.

9 It is no coincidence that Iraq, which used to have the largest military budget per head in the world, used to spend the least on human development.

10 See UN *Human Development Report*, op. cit., p. 4.

11 See Warren C. Baum and Stokes M. Tobert, *Investing in Development: Lessons of World Bank Experience*, New York, Oxford University Press, 1985, p. 275.

12 See UN *Human Development Report*, op. cit., p. 6.

13 Let me digress for a moment. When Third World countries appoint 'experts' to ministerial positions – an electrical engineer for the Ministry of Electricity, a doctor for the Ministry of Health – they are following a policy which is far from sound. By the very nature of things, a minister who is an expert will concentrate on his field of expertise. In other words, he will interfere in purely technical matters which are best left to technicians and neglect the 'broader issues' which should be the prime concern of a minister. It is no business of a Minister of Electricity to design power-stations, just as it is not the business of a Minister of Health to lay down specifications for hospitals. Their main task is to ensure that the service reaches the largest percentage of the population at the lowest cost.

14 Galal Amin's comment is that Arab architecture was unable to distinguish between 'the Alpine climate of Mount Lebanon and the furnace heat of Kuwait'. See his, *The Modernization of Poverty*, Leiden, E. J. Brill, 1974, p. 113.

15 See Abdullah al-Khariji, *Experiences of Development in the Arab World: A Study of Displacement and Settlement Processes*, Jeddah, Dar al-Shuruq, AH1400/AD1980, p. 75.

16 Few Arabs are ashamed of the close ties which have existed throughout history between the Arabs and the camel, a noble beast which has played a major role in Arab life and the spread of Arab civilization. In the West people feel no embarrassment about keeping mice, snakes and various reptiles for pets.

17 Though the Shah of Iran was a clever man who was prepared to spend hours learning the technical details of subjects which were of

interest to him (e.g. he was an expert of the first order in oil, military and industrial matters), he was unable to see beyond the detail to the broader picture. When he came to Saudi Arabia on an official visit during the 1970s, I remember asking him what he thought about the fierce competition that Saudi and Iranian petrochemicals would face from the traditional producers in Europe. I was surprised when he replied flatly: 'There is no problem. They will just have to shut up shop and make way for our products.' Just how they were to be persuaded to close down their plants, the Shah did not say.

18 See Rasyard Kapuscinski, *Shah of Shahs*, London, Quartet Books, 1985, pp. 57–8.

19 The Gulf countries made a good start with planning at the beginning of the 1970s. However, increasing financial resources soon created a general and mistaken impression that planning was unimportant. By the beginning of the 1980s, planning had lost its role in these countries and the logical result can be seen in the economic difficulties which emerged at the end of the decade.

CHAPTER 5

DEVELOPMENT: THE MAGIC KEY

*Those among them with
powers of reasoning
would have fathomed the
matter out.*

The Qur'an

DEVELOPMENT:
THE MAGIC KEY

In the previous chapters, we tried to answer the four main questions: Why do we develop? For whom do we develop? What do we develop? How do we develop? But there remains a factor which is also necessary for the success of the development process. This is a certain 'mentality'. Once we are sure that it is present, we can leave it to take care of the details, confident that it will enable the right answers to be found. However, without this mentality, it is impossible to succeed in solving the problems which form an integral part of any development transformation.

Dr Hassan Sa'b wrote:

The main psychological trait of backwardness is imitation whereas the main psychological trait of progress is innovation. Of necessity, backward countries must draw their inspiration from the ideas first formulated by the developed countries, whether in technology or ideology. However, if we borrow, we must do so creatively. If we borrow blindly, we will only sink further into backwardness instead of freeing ourselves from it . . . The first means by which to liberate ourselves from backwardness is to uncover the miracles of scientific progress and to apply them in a new, systematic and constructive way to the organization of life. Such an open mind has nothing to do with the ideological mentality, which sees an idea but not its relationship to reality and application. Nor does it have anything to do with the pragmatic mentality which sees reality and application but recognizes no idea from before or after. No, it is the mentality of the social development engineer, the pioneer of progress.'[1]

A Western scholar observed:

The nearest thing there is to a single basic factor which the development process cannot dispense with is the capacity of a state to absorb the discoveries of modern science and the creativity to benefit from these innovations in the market.[2]

The mentality required is, primarily, scientific, i.e. one which relies on scientific methods to solve problems instead of groping for solutions without any method at all or blindly turning to ideology. At the same time, this scientific attitude must recognize reality and the limits and constraints which it imposes. This mentality does not hesitate to borrow whatever is of benefit or to reject whatever is harmful. It does not strive after the new because it is seduced by novelty nor shrink from the old because it has been done before. In this mentality, there is no place for parrot-like repetition. The set of intellectual traits and attributes needed for success in development work we might term 'the development mentality'.

The development mentality stands in contradiction to a

delusion widely prevalent in virtually every Third World country, namely that money is the sole factor in the development equation and that a trip to the bank or the Ministry of Finance is the first step in any development process. The fact of the matter is that extremely important aspects of development have nothing to do with money at all. The best example of this is freedom. In one country after another, practical experience has shown that raising the level of freedom generally raises the level of human development.[4] It is obvious that freedom is not some project with an economic cost which can be calculated. Experience has also shown that most countries have the capacity to use their existing resources more efficiently by following co-operative development methods and applying joint venture programmes,[5] i.e. using methods which do not entail financial consequences of any kind.

During the 1980s, the Saudi Ministry of Health succeeded in introducing rapid and exciting improvements in the level of medical services with the help of monitoring by the people themselves. A 24-hour hotline was set up in the Ministry to receive complaints from the public. This measure proved more effective than employing hundreds of official inspectors. Public committees, known as 'Friends of the Patient', were set up in every region. They make unannounced visits to hospitals to see that patients are well looked after and to check the level of services provided. The results gradually achieved by these committees have been greater than those of the official inspectorate. These suggestions came from colleagues when I was Minister of Health. (This is further proof of the effectiveness of decentralized management.)

The development mentality refuses to leave the whole burden of development on the State and recognizes the major role which can be played by individuals and private organizations. The view that the State is everything in the development equation may have been acceptable when the propaganda machine of the socialist regimes was able to cover up the shortcomings of the

State. However, now that the socialist regimes have been revealed as bankrupt, it would be wrong to cling to such a view. Encouraging the private sector to provide medical and educational services to those who can afford them is one way of relieving the pressure on official institutions and enabling them to improve services provided for those who are less well-off.

It would be inefficient for the State to retain ownership of all economic institutions when they can be privatized and made to provide a better service at lower cost. The present wayward situation in some countries, in which the State tries to act as farmer or trader, continues for one reason and for one reason only: the all-pervasive bureaucracy refuses to yield an inch in the struggle to cling on to its empire.

With the development mentality, projects can be carried out at the lowest possible cost instead of the high costs currently being paid throughout the Third World. In the field of education, some 25 per cent could be cut from the total bill through a series of innovative measures, such as a greater use of local resources, more classes, a selective increase in class size, the adoption of a system which would recoup some of the costs of higher education, using teaching assistants who require less training than regular teachers, etc.[6] Interesting results have been achieved by applying these principles. In Bangladesh, the annual cost of primary education in private schools is only 15 dollars per child.[7] In Saudi Arabia, great savings were made when the Ministry of Education decided to build simpler schools using local methods and materials.

In the field of health services, costs can be reduced considerably. First of all, the focus of attention must be shifted from high-cost remedial medicine to low-cost preventive medicine. The cost of a single cardiac clinic is enough to build dozens of primary health-care centres (without which it is impossible to get rid of any illness, including heart disease). It is also possible to achieve substantial savings in the cost of drugs, where waste accounts for as much as 70 per cent in some countries. In the Gulf States, where medical services are free, a patient will often go from one doctor to another within the same hospital and leave loaded down with expensive medicines which are then not used or which may even be thrown away. In front of the gates of almost every Gulf hospital, the passer-by will find mounds of discarded drugs. Obviously, this is a situation which could be remedied straight away by charging patients a small proportion of the cost of the medicine. Estimates suggest that per capita consumption of medicine in the developing countries, which amounted to US$5.40 in 1985, could be reduced to US$1.00 by eliminating some medicines or to US$0.25 if only the most vital drugs were dispensed.[8]

What is true for reducing costs in the fields of education and health is also true for other development fields. For example, the cost of obtaining drinking-water can be reduced through modern technology, provided that it is combined with an appropriate administrative structure. For example, it is possible to improve wells and the pumps to draw water from narrow wells at costs ranging from just five dollars to less than 50 cents per user.[9] In every area of public services, substantial cost savings can be obtained by adopting the right methods.[10] In Saudi Arabia, some ministries have been able to reduce project costs by a third through eliminating non-essential specifications and broadening the base of competition so as to allow Asian companies to compete with Western ones.

With the development mentality, it is possible to raise the efficiency of a service while reducing costs. Perhaps the best illustration of what can be achieved in this field can be seen in the field of health care in China. Doctors require long years of training at vast expense and, as often happens in the Third World, they settle in the towns, leaving the villages with little or no health provision. The Chinese found a radical solution to this problem by giving groups of young people short and simple training in the treatment of contagious and endemic diseases, providing them with the necessary medicines and then sending them out into the countryside. These 'barefoot doctors' roamed the whole country and in no time had managed to eliminate disease and to solve the day-to-day health problems of the people. It is regrettable that this great pioneering experiment has not been repeated throughout the Third World, despite the unparalleled success achieved wherever it has been tried. For example, despite the fact that Sri Lanka is an extremely poor country, it was able to bring life expectancy up to US levels by making use of the Chinese method.[11]

Singapore's solution to its transport problems is an outstanding example of the development mentality at work. Instead of using the palliatives and symbolic gestures so common in Third World countries when they are faced with problems of this kind, Singapore devised a solution that was comprehensive, radical and multi-faceted. The whole city centre was transformed into a car park and anyone who parked had to pay a progressively rising charge. A public transport system was established, consisting mainly of buses, and the flow of traffic was organized and improved. In parallel with these measures, the number of vehicles and the ways in which they are used was controlled by taxation. A long-term policy was adopted to provide employment opportunities close to new residential areas and away from the city centre. The end-result of all these decisions was to defuse the crisis, to allow traffic to flow smoothly and to reduce pollution levels.[12]

Singapore was also able to deal with one of the most serious problems facing the Third World – some people would say the most serious problem of all – namely the population explosion. The solutions put forward were many, ranging from the repressive, i.e. imposed from above, to the optional, i.e. teaching people about the scale of the problem. However, these solutions met with only limited success. The problem is closely related to people's religious beliefs, customs and traditions so that it is difficult to deal with it by decree or by advice. In order to avoid any clash with tradition and custom, Singapore used the innovative method of charging for the issue of birth certificates on a progressive scale: the first was free, the second was charged a small sum, while the fee charged for the third rose steeply. This approach was so successful that, for a short time, the problem switched from the danger of overpopulation to a fall in demographic rates that threatened the future existence of the country.

While the development mentality advocates innovative solutions rather than old remedies which have proved to be a failure, it does not discard tried and tested answers simply for the sake of finding something new. The criterion by which any solution is to be judged is not whether it is old or new but whether it is effective. For example, Sri Lanka made great strides in the field of health care by combining the services of traditional healers with those of modern medicine. (In most Third World countries, the trend has been just the opposite: the doctors responsible for the provision of health care are hostile to traditional medicine, which they see as a field for quacks and charlatans.)[13] In a number of countries of the Arabian Peninsula, grazing land used to be protected by the age-old tribal system. With the passing of this tradition, the soil deteriorated, the environment was damaged and livestock suffered.

When I say that we must retain and not let go of any tried and tested method, I am reminded of a PhD thesis written by a Western scholar on Saudi Arabia's organization of the pilgrimage to Mecca. He concluded that, if any industrialized country tried to handle a comparable influx of visitors within the same period of time, there would be a complete collapse of all public services. He also concluded that the success of the kingdom in coping with the enormous number of pilgrims was due to the use of ways and means which had proved their worth over long years of practice and that introducing modern management methods to replace the old ones would lead to insoluble problems.

In this context, it is puzzling to see Third World countries vying with each other to acquire computers, even when there is no logical reason for using them. It may be that computers are necessary for managing the accounts of banks, for airline bookings and complex industrial projects, but it is hard to see why computers are needed to prepare salaries in a ministry where the financial department already employs hundreds of staff to do just that. Automation becomes a curse rather than a blessing when employees whose services are no longer needed are not trained to do other work. An excessive use of automation in the West has led to the strange phenomenon of work being taken away from people and given to machines. If one thing is certain, it is that this trend has nothing to recommend it to the Third World. It must also be noted here that the countries which import computers do not import the maintenance service to go with them. How often when we are waiting for a service do we hear the words, 'Sorry, the computer's out of order!'. We pay for performance but we do not get it. In many Third World capitals, the computer is little more than a status symbol and has nothing at all to do with efficiency.

The development mentality does not recognize 'the most expensive technology' or the 'the latest technology' – which usually means the same thing. The only one it does recognize is 'the most appropriate technology'. It is often the case that the Third World's obsession with acquiring the latest (and most expensive) technologies leads to negative results. Let us take sugar production as an example. We can establish a giant ultra-modern plant with a capacity of 12,000 tonnes, providing employment for less than a thousand workers. For the same price, we could build fifty smaller factories with a capacity of 3,000 tonnes, providing employment for many times that number of workers.[14] If the latest technologies in the field of agriculture, such as sophisticated ploughing equipment, are used in an environment which is unsuitable due to the small scale, the number of owners, the nature of the soil, etc., this may lead to the precise opposite of the desired result.[15] The sewage systems used in the industrialized world are designed on the basis of the availability of large quantities of water. When these systems are imported without modification into the Third World, complications arise because the water supply is inadequate.[16] In many Third World countries, the use of heavy machinery soon leads to a deterioration in roads not designed to bear its weight. This, in turn, leads to damage to the equipment itself.

With the development mentality, a lot can be achieved when emphasis is placed on the technology which is appropriate for the environment. A perfect example in this context is the potential available in the energy field. Research shows that the Third World could provide villages and rural areas with cheaper and more efficient lighting than that provided by power-stations, through the use of localized alternatives such as solar power, waterfalls, fuelwood and dung. China has achieved great successes in this field. By the late 1970s, it had some seven million biogas units producing power from dung and some 88,000 units generating electricity from local waterfalls.[17]

The development mentality does not seek 'quick' solutions unless speed is accompanied by efficiency. In Saudi Arabia during the 1970s, many bottlenecks arose because the basic infrastructure could not cope. People clamoured for 'urgent solutions' and, because the country had the necessary financial resources, the demands could be met. Thus, alongside the long-term solutions, urgent solutions were found in every field: prefabricated accommodation was provided until permanent housing was completed; electricity generators were distributed until the national grid was finished; temporary quays were erected in the ports while the permanent structures were being constructed. The urgent solution fever reached its height when helicopters were brought in to unload cargoes! In almost every case, experience has shown that urgent solutions are a waste of money and effort. Moreover, some of them make the problem worse rather than better.

If the development mentality is so awesomely effective, if it can solve problems wherever they arise and if problems arise when it is absent, why is it not to be found throughout the Third World? The answer is that the development mentality is intimately bound up with education, which, in turn, is inextricably linked with the educational system. So tragic is the state of education in Third World countries, that even their enemies must be moved to pity. It is perhaps here that we shall find the 'magic key' to development: the key without which it is impossible to achieve development, even if all the other necessary elements are present. This magic key is education.

The most serious deficiency in Third World education is that, after so many years of independence, it has completely failed to eradicate illiteracy. At a time when illiteracy has virtually disappeared from the industrialized countries, we find that illiteracy rates in some Third World countries are still over 50 per cent in some and 70 per cent in others. In the Arab world, for example, illiteracy rates remain so frighteningly high that one study was prompted to remark that 'three-quarters of the population of the Arab world place a serious burden on the progress of Arab development'.[18]

The correlation between illiteracy and backwardness, and resulting low productivity, hardly requires proof. It has been shown that a farm labourer who has had four years of education is 13 per cent more productive than one who is illiterate. It has also been shown that fathers and mothers who have completed primary education are better able to apply the principles of good nutrition and hygiene than illiterate parents. Indeed, some studies have indicated that there is a direct correlation between the level of education of the mother and the life expectancy of her children.[19]

At a time when the educational system in the Third World is unable to eradicate illiteracy, it is placing a disproportionate emphasis on university education, thus compounding one error with another. The establishment of universities without aim or co-ordination leads not to an increase in the educational level of the workforce but to graduate unemployment. In Sri Lanka, for example, 90 per cent of job-seekers during the 1970s were young people under the age of 20 with higher educational qualifications.[20] In India, during the same period, there were 2.3 million university graduates seeking work.[21] The phenomenon of graduate unemployment – with all the implications this has for political and social stability – is now widespread in all the capitals of the Third World.

The educational systems which have failed to put an end to illiteracy or to put university education on the right track have also failed to provide society with the trained manpower it needs.[22] These failures stem from the fact that the systems themselves are obsolete, the vestiges of an educational structure created by the colonial powers to turn out low-level clerks in the days before development. When independence came, it was attended by highflown slogans but no new vision to revise the old educational system. (Everywhere the 'inspired leaders' were too busy pursuing their 'appointments with destiny' to find time for such a 'trivial' matter as education, which was left to second-rate officials.) After independence, things remained as they had been before: the role of primary schools was to prepare pupils for secondary school; secondary schools were there to prepare them for university; the universities were there to turn out civil servants. Under this extraordinary system, the State apparatus was crammed with vast numbers of unnecessary civil servants while agriculture and industry were crying out for skilled labour such as nurses, plumbers, joiners and metalworkers. Under this system, graduate unemployment went hand in hand with a scarcity of people with manual skills.

It should now be apparent that it is impossible to attain the development mentality (i.e. to attain development) unless there is a root-and-branch reform of the educational systems in the Third World. The first aim of reform must be to eradicate illiteracy completely and to provide each child with compulsory basic education for a period of not less than nine years. The second aim must be to ensure that there is a perfect match between the requirements of development and the curricula, so that programmes meet the needs of society by providing the necessary skills for development to succeed. The third aim is to do away with ineffective teaching[23] and to make use of the very latest methods devised by pedagogical science for instruction and training. The educational system must provide its services to everyone, firstly to the poor. It must abandon the favouritism – manifest throughout the Third World – which gives privileges to the wealthy at the expense of all other classes.

Though the required reforms are profound and far-reaching, they are not impossible to achieve, if the determination to attain development is there. We have only to look at the experience of South Korea, which is rapidly transforming itself from an under-developed country into an advanced one. Korea has made great strides in the field of education, eradicating illiteracy, introducing compulsory education and requiring vocational trainees to spend several years in general education before entering vocational training centres.[24] The result has been a substantial increase in productivity in every area of the economy.

Due attention must be paid to scientific research in the reform of the educational system. At present, Third World spending on applied research is no more than 5 per cent of the amount spent by the industrialized countries.[25] Even this low figure comes almost entirely from a small group of relatively advanced countries, such as India, Brazil and Mexico. Moreover, many of the studies carried out in the industrialized world have nothing whatsoever to do with the Third World. What is needed are solutions through applied research in each country. In this regard, it should be noted that no development of any significance has been achieved in the treatment of tropical diseases because it is not a health priority in the industrialized world. On the other hand, vast amounts are spent on research into finding a cure for diabetes, which is not considered to be a health problem in the Third World. Due attention to scientific research may be the first effective step towards halting the brain drain which deprives the Third World of the cream of its talents and which has become so serious that the Third World is now exporting skills to the industrialized countries instead of importing them. In many industrialized countries, medical services rely to a large extent on doctors who have emigrated from the Third World.[26]

Let me now bid the reader farewell with one final recommendation, a conclusion that I have arrived at after quarter of a century of practical and theoretical involvement in development. It is this: the road to development starts with education and ends with education. Education is the first word and the last word in the epic struggle for development.[27]

NOTES

1 Hassan Sa'b, *Modernization of the Arab Mind*, Beirut, 3rd edn, Dar al-'Ilm li'l-Malayin, 1980, p. 57.

2 Ibid., p. 60.

3 See Malcolm Gillis *et al.*, *Economics of Development*, New York, W. W. Norton & Co., 1983, p. 20.

4 See *UN Human Development Report for 1991*, New York, Oxford University Press, p. 14.

5 Ibid., p. 2.

6 Ibid., p. 86.

7 Ibid., p. 86.

8 Ibid., p. 7.

9 Ibid., p. 88.

10 Ibid., pp. 88–95.

11 See Colin Norman, *The God that Limps: Science and Technology in the Eighties*, New York, W. W. Norton & Co., 1981, p. 166.

12 See Warren C. Baum and Stokes M. Tobert, *Investing in Development: Lessons of World Bank Experience*, New York, Oxford University Press, 1985, p. 299.

13 At a time when the West is beginning to recognize 'alternative medicine', including homoeopathy and acupuncture, doctors responsible for health care in the Third World still regard alternative medicine with a hostility.

14 Norman, op. cit., p. 63.

15 See Uma Lele, *The Design of Rural Development: Lessons from Africa*, Baltimore, Md., Johns Hopkins University Press, 1975, p. 33.

16 Norman, op. cit., p. 168.

17 Ibid., p. 170.

18 Tayyib Tayzini *et al.*, *Arab Development Planning: Horizons and Limits*, Pt. 2: Sectoral Topics, Kuwait, Kazima Publishing & Translating Co., 1981, p. 24.

19 See Baum and Tolbert, op. cit., p. 120.

20 See Ozay Mehemet, *Economic Planning and Social Justice in Developing Countries*, New York, St Martin's Press, 1978, p. 89.

21 See Nath Varma Baiydia, *The Sociology and Politics of Development: A Theoretical Study*, London, Routledge & Kegan Paul, 1980, p. 111.

22 In 1980, whereas a country the size of Indonesia had no more than thirty MBAs, a company like IBM could employ more than a thousand of them.

23 At the present time, education throughout the Third World relies on 'teaching methods in which the teacher, who knows everything, takes the active role and imparts knowledge unidirectionally to the student, who knows nothing. A passive role is imposed on the student, who is given no opportunity to participate, discuss or practise. The end-result is that, at best, the student learns without understanding. He prepares for examinations but, as a person, he remains uneducated.' Mustafa Hijazi, *Social Backwardness: An Introduction to the Psychology of the Downtrodden*, 1st edn, Beirut, Arab Development Institute, 1976, p. 113.

24 See Wahba Handusa, 'Management of economic development in South Korea', *Independent Development in the Arab World*, Beirut Centre for Arab Unity Studies, 1987, pp. 365–97.

25 According to an Arab researcher: 'We [the Arabs] are the most miserly people on earth towards our scientists. In North America, US$76,000 per annum is spent on every scientist, in Europe, US$75,000, in Asia, US$45,000 and in Africa, US$51,000. In the Arab world, however, the figure is just US$30,000!' See Usama al-Khalidi, 'Arab efforts in the basic sciences', *Al-Arabi*, 346 (Sept. 1987), pp. 57–63.

26 Queen Elizabeth II once told me that she was happy to see non-British staff working in the British hospitals she visited but she was

also sad about the shortages which their departure left in their home countries.

27 Let us recall here that, Taha Hussein, that great pioneer of development in the 1930s and 1940s, maintained that education was as important to man as food, drink and the air he breathes.

REFERENCES

ARABIC LANGUAGE REFERENCES

Abdulaziz Abdullah al-Jalal, *Cultivating Prosperity and Retarding Development*, Kuwait, 'Alam al-Ma'rifa, 1985.

Abdullah Al-Khariji, *Some Experiences in Development in the Arab World: Studies in Displacement and Settlement*, Jeddah, Dar al-Shuruq, AH1400/AD1980.

Abdulmajid Farid, *Arabs with no Oil*, Beirut, Institute of Arab Studies, 1986.

Ali Shariati, *Return to Self*, trans. by Ibrahim al-Dasuqi Shatta, Cairo, al-Zahra li'l-I'lam al-Arabi, 1986.

Centre for Arab Unity Studies, *Arab Development: The Present Reality and the Future*, Beirut, 1984.

—*Independent Development in the Arab World*, Beirut, 1987.

George Karam, *Development Lost: Studies in the Crisis of Arab Civilisation and Development*, Beirut, Dar al-Tali'a for Printing and Publishing, 1985.

Ghazi Abdulrahman Algosaibi, *Face to Face with Development*, Jeddah, Tihama, AH1410/AD1989.

Hassan Sa'b, *Modernization of the Arab Mind*, Beirut, Dar al-'Ilm li'l-Malayin, 1980.

Hazim al-Bablawi, *Observations on the Contemporary Economic Reality*, Kuwait, Kitab al-Arabi, 1986.

Khairi Aziz, *Issues of Development and Modernization in the Arab World, Egypt and the Maghrib*, Beirut, Dar al-Afaaq al-Jadida, 1983.

Khalid Muhammad Khalid, *Islamiyat*, Beirut, Dar al-Fikr, AH1398/AD1978.

Mahmud Al-Hamsi, *Development Plans in the Countries of the Arab Gulf and Arab Economic Integration*, Beirut, Ma'had al-Inma' al-Arabi, 1982.

Mahmud Muhammad Safar, *Development is an Issue*, Jeddah, Tihama, AH1400/AD1980.

Mahmud al-Sadani, *al-Musawwir*, Feb. 1990, p. 82.

Muhammad Fayiz, *Problems of Development in the Third World*, Riyadh, Dar al-Watan, AH1404/AD1984.

Muhammad Hasanain Haikal, *History Revisited*, Beirut, Printing, Distribution and Publishing Company, 1987.

Muhammad Shawqi Al-Fanjari, 'Man's right under Islam to a decent standard of living', *Human Rights Journal*, 8/7 (1990), pp. 45–52.

Muhyi al-Din Sabir, *Cultural Change and Development of Society*, Beirut, al-Maktaba al-'Asriya, 1962.

Mustafa Hijazi, *Social Underdevelopment: An Introduction to the Psychology of the Downtrodden*, Beirut, Ma'had Al-Inma' al-arabi, 1976.

National Institute for Planning, Kuwait, *Seminar on National Planning Methodology and the Preparation of Joint Arab Projects*, Kuwait, 1983.

Ramzi Zaki, 'Writing off Third World debt is a necessity and not an option', *al-Arabi*, Nov. 1989, p. 26.

Sa'd al-Din Ibrahim, *The New Arab Social System*, Beirut, Centre for Arab Unity Studies, 1982.

Samir Abduh, *Modernizing the Arab Nation*, Beirut, Dar al-Afaaq al-Jadida, AH1401/AD1981.

Samuel Abboud, *Five Main Problems for a Backward World*, Beirut, Dar al-Hadatha for Printing, Publishing and Distribution, 1983.

al-Suyuti, *History of the Caliphs*, Cairo, al-Maktaba al-Tijariyya al-Kubra, 1952.

Tayyib Tayzini *et al.*, *Planning for an Arab Development: Scope and Limits*, Kuwait, Kazima Publishing & Translation Company, 1981.

References

Usama al-Khaldi, 'Arab efforts in the basic sciences', *al-Arabi*, Sept. 1987, pp. 57–63.

ENGLISH LANGUAGE REFERENCES

Agarwala, Ramgopal, *Planning in Developing Countries: Lessons of Experience*, World Bank, Staff Working Papers, No. 576, 1983.

Amin, Galal, *The Modernization of Poverty*, Leiden, E .J. Brill. 1974.

Baidya, Nath Verma, *The Sociology and Politics of Development*, London, Routledge & Kegan Paul, 1980.

Bauer, P. T., *Equality, the Third World and Economic Delusion*, Cambridge, Mass., 1983.

Baum, Warren C., and Tobet, Stokes M., *Investing in Development: Lesson of World Bank Experience*, New York, Oxford University Press, 1985.

The Brandt Commission, Common Crisis: *North-South Cooperation for World Recovery*, Cambridge, Mass., 1983.

Down, Anthony, *Inside Bureaucracy*, Boston, Little, Brown & Co., 1967.

Drucker, Peter F., *Technology, Management and Society*, New York, Harper & Row, 1967.

Frank, André Gunder, *Critique and Anti-Critique*, New York, Praeger, 1984.

Gillis, Malcolm *et al.*, *Economics of Development*, New York, W. W. Norton & Co., 1983.

The Global 2000 Report to the President, New York, Penguin Books, 1987.

Gould, David J., and Ramo-Reyes, José A., *The Effects of Corruption on Administrative Performance: Illustrations from Developing Countries*, World Bank, Staff Working Papers, No. 580, p. 8.

Graham, Robert, *Iran: The Illusion of Power*, London, Croom Helm, 1978.

Hardiman, Margaret, and Midgley, James, *The Social Dimensions of Development*, New York, John Wiley & Sons Ltd, 1982.

Higgot, Richard A., *Political Development Theory*, New York, St Martin's Press, 1989.

Hilhors, J. G. M., and Keater, M., *Social Development in the Third World*, London, Croom Helm, 1985.

Ingolf, V. and de Souza, A. R., *Dialectics of Third World Development*, Osum Publishers, 1980.

Kapuscinski, Rasyard, *Shah of Shahs*, London, Quartet Books, 1985.

Lall, Sanjaya, and Stewart, Francis, *Theory and Reality in Development*, New York, St Martin's Press, 1986.

Lele, Uma, *The Designs of Rural Development: Lessons from Africa*, Baltimore, Md., Johns Hopkins University Press, 1978.

Lewis, John P., and Kallab, Valeriane, *Development Strategies Reconsidered*, Oxford, Transaction Books, 1986.

Lombardi, Richard W., *Debt Trap: Rethinking the Logic of Development*, New York, Praeger, 1985.

Mehemet, Ozay, *Economic Planning and Social Justice in Developing Countries*, New York, St Martin's Press, 1978.

Meier, Gerald M., and Seers, Dudley, *Pioneers in Development*, Oxford University Press Publication for the World Bank, 1984.

Morris, David, *Measuring the Conditions of the World's Poor*, New York, Pergamon Press, 1979.

Norman, Colin, *The God that Limps: Science and Technology in the Eighties*, New York, W. W. Norton & Co., 1981.

Robertson, A. F., *People and the State*, Cambridge University Press, 1984.

Rostow, W. W., *Politics and the Stages of Growth*, Cambridge University Press,1971.

Servan-Schreiber, Jean-Jaques, *The World Challenge*, New York, Simon

References

& Schuster, 1980.

Streeten, P. *et al.*, *First Things First*, Oxford University Press Publication for the World Bank, 1981.

Ul-Haq, Mahboub, *The Poverty Curtain*, New York, Columbia University Press,1976.

United Nations, *Annual Development Reports*.

Van Nieawenhuijse, C. A. O., *Development Begins at Home*, Pergamon Press, 1982.

Walton, J., *Reluctant Rebels*, New York, Columbia University Press,1984.